"They dined on mince, and slices of quince,
 Which they ate with a runcible spoon;
And hand in hand, on the edge of the sand,
 They danced by the light of the moon"

EDWARD LEAR (1867)

THE
COMPLETE
BOOK
OF
MINCE

THE COMPLETE BOOK OF
MINCE

René La Sagne

Cordon Brun Recipes For All The Family

REALLY
MINCEY

Waverley Books

The Complete Book of Mince by René La Sagne

First published 2008, by Waverley Books,
David Dale House,
New Lanark,
ML11 9DJ, Scotland

With special thanks to John Abernethy
and Hugo Breingan
Cookery consultants: Louise Sinclair
and Alexa Munro
Editor: Eleanor Abraham
Designer: Mark Mechan

ISBN 978 1 902407 74 6

Printed and bound in the EU

Typeset in Bitstream Futura BT

A catalogue for this book is
available from the British Library

1 2 3 4 5 6 7 8 9 10

FOREWORD

BY FOOD CRITIC, HORACE AFFAMÉ

FOR many years I have admired mince. I have eaten it, cooked it and, to be quite frank, I have lived it. It has played such a huge part in my life that I would have been idiotic, foolish and stupid, nay, even daft to have turned down the chance to write the foreword to René's wonderful collection of mince recipes.

What a guy – I have know him for about five days now and I really can say he is one of my dearest, dearest friends. And what a cook! What a guy! The food, the restaurant, the waiters, the bus stop right outside – all wholly exceptional. Paisley's public transport system is really fantastic and I am amazed every time I go there. I don't even bother to get taxis now, it is so good. And the trains to Glasgow, so regular.

But what to say about René? Well where can I start? What a guy! His floors are spotless and his wife is beautiful. I cannot fault them. I have never eaten in his restaurant but I have looked through the window as I passed it on Paisley's magnificent bus service on the way to the town centre. Do you know I can get a super-saver bus pass for £4.50? It really is outstanding value for money. The restaurant looks so classy and I bet if I did ever eat there it would be truly magnifique!

A mince restaurant, how unique! What a guy! Imagine thinking that one up! That guy has never failed to amaze me in all the hours I have known him.

And a mince cookbook? OK, that's not so unique, but it is deliciously nostalgic, truly harking back to the glorious British cuisine of the seventies. It makes me think of my own student cookery, my own dear mother's favourites and the gravy-encrusted casserole dishes of yesteryear that one can never get properly clean. Ah, will the memories never end, please?

But as for René – what a guy! And the mince! He only sells mince – and what mince it is, I expect.

I can honestly say his restaurant is truly 100% mince!!

That will be £500.

Horace Affamé

CONTENTS

*Opposite: Tatties and mince can be a romantic dish. I proposed
to my Kelly over a stuffed tomato.*

Opposite: My head waiter Serge likes to be quite dramatic when serving mince at table. The white gloves were his idea

INTRODUCTION

MY LIFE IS MINCE

MINCE changed my life. As my father-in-law from Paisley always says, over his bowl of tatties and mince, "There are as many ways to cook mince as there are ways to live, but I like mine boiled." It's better for his wallies.

Mince put me on the culinary map. Myself, René La Sagne, I come from a little place called Filo-et-Choux-sur-L'Eau in the municipality of La Sagne, in the district of La Chaux-de-Fonds, Switzerland, where there was no mince. La Sagne was a minceless municipality. There were lakes and mountains, triangular chocolate bars, and cuckoo clocks, but no mince. Nothing. Zut alors. Dull? It was pure mince, but without the mince.

So from whence did mince enter my life?

Three life-changing events transformed me. First, I was thrown into a Swiss lake by an angry park-keeper as punishment for not observing the sign, and keeping off the grass. Switzerland is a precise, literal sort of place and I was indeed off the grass at that point. Once in the freezing water, I instinctively swam. I had adapted with ease. I realised I had a gift. Had I not been adaptable, I would be no more. Drowned. Passé and blessé. Mince for the bottom feeders. I realised I was capable of anything. Many other chefs have this same philosophy.

My second miracle was the first big cultural change in my young life. Seeking to free myself from apron strings, small town sensibilities, the cuckoos, psychotic park-keepers, and the like, I went to the big city – Paris – and it was here that I found my first love – cooking. I trained in the finest Parisian restaurants, learning from the best. It was a thrilling life with long hours, physical and mental cruelty, sleep deprivation, and no time to myself.

The third miracle happened to me while on a rare holiday to Sharm El Sheikh, having been sacked from the restaurant for taking a lunch break. As always, I adapted to my new surroundings with ease – this time to the heat, and to the many accents and camels. At around 3am one day, I bumped into Kelly-Marie. As I helped her up from the floor, it was the cupid at first sight. I knew I would follow this "stoater" to the ends of the earth. But, thankfully, I only had to go as far as Paisley.

Not only was she a looker, but she was a cooker too, and she took me home, and taught me mince. I was a highly trained but sacked chef, so, with the support of her friends and family, Kelly-Marie kindly helped me find work in Paisley. Paisley became my most beloved town.

And mince became my warm, family favourite. I adapted with ease again, and there I opened my restaurant, Maison de Mince, and then launched my websites MyMince.com, and MinceBook.com.

And I married my beautiful Kelly-Marie. In Paisley Abbey. It was a braw Scottish summer day with only intermittent sleet.

PEOPLE are always asking me how to select mince – what to look for. I say, "Wake up and smell the mince". For when you have control of your mince, you have control of your stomach, your taste buds and your life. You also have control of your budget, and your social life. You have a menu for life.

Mince has it all: vitamins, energy, iron, "… and fat", I hear you critics say. Well, let me counter that. Extra-lean steak mince is the answer. The word "mince" is French you know. With no irony I can tell you that "mince" is French for thin. Bien?

Mince. Is it fattening? Well, I say to you, that some of these recipes are for the wider fitting, with the elasticated waistband. But use extra lean steak mince, and you could lose weight with this book.

I could go as far as to say, you can mince yourself thin! Do not blame the mince for the obesity crisis! We watch glorious gourmet food TV programmes, espousing healthy cookery with the best organic ingredients, and then we eat a multi-pack of salt and vinegar crisps, and a microwaved ready meal, and wash it down with a bucket of wine, and we wonder why we are obese. ("Speak for yourself René," I hear you say.) We eat too many fries with the pizza, take too little exercise, and an evening around the piano after a bowl of tatties and mince is a distant fantasy. The country has gone to les chiens. In short, as the Glaswegians say, it is mince.

So it is. For Scotland should know better. She is the homeland of fabulous mince. She invented mince. Mais oui. Mince and tatties, boiled mince … you name it … I would if I could think of any more. And although the Americans might still be celebrating Independence Day – McDonald is a Scottish name – and after all, burgers are just mince. Burgers, moussaka, lasagne, mince and tatties – it's all cooking from the heart. Shepherd's pie, cottage pie, stovies, chilli con carne, succulent mince pies and pasties and mouth-watering burgers are but a few of the myriad popular dishes that contain mince as the vital ingredient.

In the *Complete Book of Mince* I have inscribed the recipes for all these wonderful dishes and sourced many, many more. These recipes range from healthy haute cuisine to the homely staples that stuck to your ribs as a child, and the traditional meals that your grand-mère might have made, to dishes that are truly *Cordon Brun*.

Of course, there are many ways to appreciate the mince. With this book, you can be a mince hero. You can be a bad boy of mince. The mince-demon, or the mince-angel. There is something here for the student, those cooking for one, or for those returning to mince after an absence. For those who enjoy the mince on a regular basis, you can be rejuvenated with fresh ways to look at mince. Mince revisited. You can become the beacon, beaming a light of warmth and creativity to friends and family.

Here I give you the freedom to go where you want, and create excellence for your loved ones, or for new "friends" from social networking websites who would have remained remote, faceless, status-updating social deviants had you not invited them round for stovies.

These recipes are formula ones, the premier division of mince, that will take you to dazzling new heights of social ease and connectivity. Here you can find mince for beginners, and mince for sophisticates, and welcome new friends to your grounded, mincey, new life.

For who can beat the welcome that glorious mince offers? Sitting around a table, with a boutcille de plonk, and a grande bowl of la bonne mince?

Je propose we can change our lives with mince. It is time for the mince grande retrospective, in which I bring you a mincey vision. Not just a cookbook, but a fusion of art and style, fashion and the full belly. A place where we can, once again – like a contented caveman who has just discovered how to grind up a leftover rump of bison – tell stories, face to face, to our kith and kin over a roaring and steaming plate of mince.

I have grown to appreciate this unsung, and some say unfashionable, source of pleasure with the help of my wife, and I hope that you too will experience the joy of mince. I hope that by plunging in this book you will once more learn to love the odour of mince.

I give you, mince.

Bon appétit! René

PART ONE

THE MAGIC OF MINCE

WHO can tell when the mincing began? It is often thought that it was the Chinese who, in the days before mincing machines and food processors, were the first to grind leftover pieces of meat and found it to be good.

All through history, meat has often been an expensive item – all around the world. Since cooking began, chefs and home cooks have been finding ways of making a little go a long way. Was it not Jesus who fed the multitudes with but five loaves and two fishes? And who is to say that he did not also have an excellent mince recipe? Not me.

Over time, herbs and seasonings were added to give added flavouring. Filling and nourishing protein-packed dishes began to be created. Soon mince became so popular that meatballs and mince pies and other tasty snacks were invented to fulfil the demand for mince throughout the day.

The Christmas mince pie with which we are familiar these days is a fruity number, but mince pies were originally created to help spin out and preserve meat for longer. Minced meats were mixed with spices (which helped act as preservatives) and, through the centuries, currants and apples and other fruit were added, until the modern Christmas mince pie consists of no minced meat whatsoever. Worry not – there are still plenty of other mince pies recipes suitable for the meat-lovers.

It is said that it was Genghis Khan and his Mongolian hordes that came up with the idea of the minced meat patty. The Mongols would pack the meat in their saddles and after a long, hard day of rape and pillage what better way to unwind than around the campfire with burgers.

Today, friends and neighbours can get together at a barbecue where delicious hamburgers and succulent kebabs can be enjoyed along with a selection of salads and cold drinks. When the Paisley weather is fine I enjoy nothing more than hosting a barbecue to celebrate and the burgers and kebabs are always incredibly popular.

Mince provided the main ingredients of the national dishes of many

Opposite: Afternoon tea at Maison de Mince

countries around the world: lasagne in Italy, moussaka in Greece, meatballs in Sweden and our very own national treasure – mince and tatties.

The invention of mincers in the 19th century to replace the traditional meat grinders of the past made mince more accessible for butchers and households alike and when free school dinners were introduced, mince became one of the most economic and popular dishes. From the many friends and diners that I have met, school dinners were either the highlight of the school day or a daily ordeal depending on the culinary skills of the school cooks.

Some people have told me that they were put off mince for life because of these experiences. For these unfortunate few, I hope I can help them rediscover the joy of mince – the *joie de mince* that was so cruelly taken from them as children.

PRIVILEGED as I am to be owner of one of Paisley's finest à la carte dining establishments I take great pride in the food that I produce for my clientèle. Preparation is vital in creating a fantastic dish. Always ensuring that the ingredients are of the best quality, that your utensils are all ready for use, that you have all the seasonings that you require to give the recipe that *joie de vivre* that the recipe requires and you make the time and take the effort to produce something truly wonderful.

First of all purchase the correct amount of mince needed for the recipe. Tell your butcher your requirements and order accordingly. If you have a mincer at home or a food processor you can mince your meat yourself, selecting the cut that you prefer – whether it be the blade, chuck, leg, clod or shin if it is beef – and you can decide how much fat or lean you require or how fine or coarse you wish your mince to be. Make sure you have removed all gristle and skin from the meat before you start mincing and when you have finished mincing ensure that you thoroughly clean your mincer. You may wish to mince your meat several times to improve the texture of the mince.

Alternatively, if you have the time or if you do not have a mincer or food processor, you can take your mince, remove all fat and gristle and cut your meat in regular-sized slices. Place slices on top of each other and cut through to make even strips. Then cut the strips into cubes, making sure that the cubes are of similar size. Spread the cubes onto a chopping board and using two heavy knives start chopping the mince – I find that listening to up-tempo music or Whitesnake helps me get in the mood as I rhythmically work on my meat. As the mince spreads out, use one of the knife blades to flip the meat over back into the centre. Keep chopping until the mince is to the texture that you prefer.

Of course you could just visit your local supermarket and buy prepared mince and not have to worry about what exactly the chuck or clod are anyway. (The chuck is from the neck to the shoulder and the clod is the neck.)

On purchasing your mince either cook that day or store in your freezer until needed, making sure that you use it before the relevant expiry date. Mince may be wonderful, but it does go off quicker than other meat. However, it is perfectly acceptable to cook your mince and then put it in your fridge for dining the following day – if you can wait that long. Please remember to thoroughly reheat the mince or mince dish.

For centuries, herbs and spices have been used to complement and accentuate the fantastic flavour of mince, and I favour promiscuous sprinkling wherever possible. Either ensure that your spice rack is well stocked, or if you do not have a spice rack then at the very least have some pepper in the cupboard.

In this section, I have brought together some recipes for the mince beginners, a few straightforward, but still extremely tasty dishes that will see your confidence soar as your journey into the world of mince has fully begun.

C'est la mince!

MINCE-COOKING TIPS

BUY good, extra lean, properly aged (while meddling Eurocrats allow it!) steak mince, preferably from a good butcher.

Use a wooden spoon to separate the particles of mince while it cooks. Opinions differ as to how to do this. Some cooks add water to their mince while raw and mash throughly, then reduce the water and fry or simply add unthickened gravy or stock. Others (including me) believe this releases too much juicy mincey goodness from the meat and leaves it pale and uninteresting in colour and texture, and prefer to frantically mash while it cooks over a high heat till it browns, and only then, once it is a delicious dark brown, add sauces or gravy and simmer.

Once browned, simmer in your sauce or gravy. Do not boil or the meat will harden – "A stew boiled is a stew spoiled."

Browning adds flavour. Mince may be cooked in its own fat if you have a good non-stick pan or pot. Excess fat can be removed at the end of the browning process for those watching their fat intake.

Portions: Allow around 125g of raw mince per person, or 150–175g for heartier appetites. If the recipe includes a lot of extra vegetables or pulses then 75g of mince per person may be sufficient. Most supermarkets sell 500g portions and the recipes in this book reflect this.

ETIQUETTE

With more and more meetings of business and romance commencing à la table, it is so, so important that the etiquette of the table is observed correctly. This first contact or impression is vital. There are many, many common mistakes from which we all should learn.

There are rules – conventions which I have observed in my training and during my travels, whether it is at breakfast, lunch or dinner. When these handy hints have been absorbed, they can be stored and applied to any event involving plates. Throughout this book you will find little gems of dining wisdom interspersed amongst my superb mince recipes, in a cute blue box.

VEGETARIAN MINCE

FOR vegetarians, my mince dishes can be made by substituting vegetarian, meat-substitute mince, such as Quorn™ or soya mince, for meat. OK, maybe not steak tartare.

And I believe there has not been much call for soya mince in a Scotch pie, but one lives in hope.

There is great call for vegetarian dishes in my restaurant as there is a high percentage of students living nearby, and I am more than happy to quickly rustle up some vegetarian stovies, etc., for the hungry little dears. Their reluctance in the tipping department, propensity to share a bowl of soup between two and divide bills into 14 does not make me bitter. They will be doctors and lawyers one day and may come back and order chateaubriand, minced of course!

Lentils, pulses and nuts can also be processed to use in lovely burgers and nut-loafs. Tinned kidney beans and chickpeas are delicious when made into a chunky paste. Lentils and pulses need not be processed for use in stews and casseroles, they are delicious whole and will break down and soften in the cooking process anyway.

If you are not a vegan you can bind processed pulses and nuts with an egg and some breadcrumbs and add seasonings and fried onions etc., as you would to any meat burger recipe. Shape, coat in breadcrumbs and shallow fry.

Soya mince may be bound with an egg and breadcrumbs and made into burgers, sausages and patties this way. Mashed potato is a good binding agent too.

I am confident you can follow many ot the meaty recipes given here, missing out meat, meat stock and gravy, or suet and replacing with Quorn™, soya mince, beans and pulses, vegetable stock and vegetable oils.

Amounts of seasoning and sauces may need to be increased, in my experience, as pulses do tend to need more flavouring. They are much lower in fat than meat, which is good, but fat does add flavour.

The following recipes will easily accomodate the substitution of exactly the same amounts of Quorn™ or soya mince for meat:

COTTAGE PIE
SHEPHERD'S PIE
BEEF HOT POT
MINCE AND MACARONI
BEEF BEANPOT
STUFFED ONIONS
STUFFED MUSHROOMS
BAKED POTATO WITH SPICED LAMB
STUFFED PEPPERS
STUFFED MARROW
MINCED BEEF WITH PASTA
SPAGHETTI BOLOGNESE
MINCED LAMB CRÊPES
LASAGNE AL FORNO
CHILLI CON CARNE
MOUSSAKA
CURRIED LAMB MINCE
CURRIED BEEF MINCE
LAMB MINCE KORMA
COUNTRY PIE
PASTIES
MINCED BEEF AND VEGETABLE PIE
BOBOTIE

Recipes that are easily adapted this way using vegetarian ingredients will be accompanied by the following symbol:

MINCE AND TATTIES

THE mashed potato and the mince – truly a match made in heaven. There are so many wonderful versions of mince and tatties that I am almost reluctant to suggest any one specific recipe. Many have been the times on my nights off from preparing gourmet cuisine at Maison de Mince that I have been fortunate enough to have been invited to dinner and eaten the most delicious mince et pomme de terres. Almost every time, there has been a subtle difference in the cooking: the colour and lumpiness of the mince, the amount of gravy granules used, the choice of vegetable accompaniments and the preferred seasoning. Friendships have been lost and families split over the controversy of the addition of la sauce "rouge" or "brun".

Much thought is given to accompaniments and some people even serve vegetables. I have found, throughout my travels through Scotland, that there is a national pride in making the perfect plate of mince and tatties, although I have yet to taste the famed Edinburgh mince and tatties as when I visit friends in the Capital they have frequently already had their tea.

Did you know that a World Mince and Tatties championship is held annually at Tobermory on the Scottish island of Mull? Entrants travel from across the globe for the opportunity to produce the greatest mince in the world.

Wester Ross Gazette
WORLD MINCE AND TATTIES CHAMPIONSHIPS

MUCH STEWING AT MINCE COMPETITION

THERE was a tense, exciting and controversial evening of top quality mince at the Ross, Cromarty and Skye heat for the Mince and Tatties World Championship that took place in front of an enthusiastic and knowledgeable audience at Plockton High School last night.

Six of the best cooks in the Highlands pitted their culinary skills against each other and against the clock to make the best Highland mince and tatties in front of judges – René La Sagne, head chef at one of Paisley's premier à la carte restaurants and renowned local food critic Donald MacDonald.

The six competitors were Mrs Shona MacGregor of Portree, Mrs Morag MacKenzie of Kyle, Mr Crawford Bruce of Achnasheen,

Miss Janet Grieve of Strathcarron, Mrs Fiona Anderson of Stromeferry and local favourite Mrs Katy Wilson of Plockton and the competition was divided into two challenges with three competitors being eliminated halfway through.

The first challenge saw the contestants make tatties in a strict thirty-minute time period. Four of the cooks went for their mashed tatties creamed, with two, Mrs MacGregor and Mrs Anderson, going for the more traditional non-creamed mashed tatties. There was some controversy when the judges stated a decided preference for creamed over non-creamed, eliminating Mrs MacGregor and Mrs Anderson, along with Mr Bruce who the judges said had used too much butter.

Tension was high as the three remaining competitors went into the final challenge of making perfect

mince and tatties in one hour. All three went for both onions and carrots in the mince and Ms Grieve added mashed neeps to her tatties. Variations took place with the amount of thickening used and, to observers, Mrs Wilson's mince was definitely thicker and darker than the other two.

On completion of the challenge, the judges tasted all three dishes and, after a long deliberation where they commended the high quality of the mince and tatties, announced Miss Grieve as the winner with Mrs MacKenzie runner-up, much to the disappointment of the local audience who felt that Mrs Wilson had been discriminated against because of the colour of her mince.

Janet Grieve will now go forward to the World Championships in Tobermory on the Isle Of Mull in two months' time.

Tatties and mince is a very special dish in Scotland — if haggis is our national dish (I feel like a Scot these days) then mince and tatties is our other national dish.

I am told that in the East coast of Scotland they have the "mince and tatties" and in the West coast they have the "tatties and mince". Are the tatties more important in the West? Is the mince more important in the East? Amazingly, no serious research has yet been done into the complex sociologial reasons for this fascinating difference. Whatever the reason, it is important to me that the mince is put on the plate first. Why? I'm not sure, it just seems right that way.

Mince has sustained generations of Scots. Most Scottish matriarchs will have a special mince pot, passed down from mother to daughter, that they will all claim imparts a distinctive, unique — and superior — familial mince flavour.

I too have a special mince pot — catering size — but unfortunately it is not one that was passed down through the family. Kelly-Marie's family's favourite dishes do not come in a pot (other than the noodles), and it is unusual for cardboard pizza boxes to survive more than one generation.

500g lean steak mince
2 onions chopped
2 carrots chopped
25g plain flour
Approx 250 ml beef stock or gravy (Some use gravy powder. Zut! If using gravy powder omit the flour.)

Mash the mince to separate the pieces and then brown it thoroughly over a high heat. Browning adds flavour. It may be browned in a non-stick pot using its own fat. Once browned, add the chopped onions and cook on a lower heat till they are soft.

Chop the carrots into circles — they taste best this way as the sweet inner core is intact in each slice — and add to the mince. Add the flour and mix thoroughly. Add enough beef stock or good gravy to cover the mince. Simmer till the mince is tender and the carrots are soft and the gravy is nice and thick — about an hour.

Serve with floury potatoes, mashed till smooth with milk and butter.

Opposite: My signature dish, tatties and mince

COTTAGE PIE

Cottage pie is a traditional dish of minced beef. The beef in the pie may have been left over from the Sunday roast. It is baked with buttery mashed potato on top. In Australia and New Zealand the cottage pie is called a potato pie or potato-top pie and in America it is sometimes called a cowboy pie.

You do not have to live in a cottage to make cottage pie.

500g minced beef
1 onion, diced
1 carrot , diced
Beef stock or gravy, about 1 cup
Salt and pepper
6 large potatoes, boiled, mashed and cooled
25g butter

Brown the minced beef thoroughly. Add the onion and carrot and fry until soft. Add about a cup of beef stock or gravy to a moist but not too runny consistency. Add salt and pepper. Place in a pie-dish and top the pie with a thick crust of cooled mashed potatoes. Use a fork that has been dipped in hot water to mark the crust. Dot the crust with butter and bake for 40 minutes at 190°C, 380°F or gas mark 5 until brown.

Other ingredients a cottage pie can include are garlic, herbs, peas and other vegetables.

SHEPHERD'S PIE

Shepherd's pie is a variation of the cottage pie but usually consists of minced lamb rather than minced beef. You do not have to be a shepherd to make a shepherd's pie.

500g minced lamb
1 onion, sliced in circles
Salt and pepper
Lamb stock or good gravy, about 1 cup
6 large potatoes, boiled, mashed and cooled
25g butter

Brown the minced lamb in its own fat. Add the onion and fry until soft. Place in a pie-dish. Add enough gravy or stock to moisten, but don't make it too runny. Cover with cold mashed potatoes. Dot potatoes with butter and bake for 40 minutes at 190°C, 375°F, gas mark 5 until brown.

ETIQUETTE: IN POLITE COMPANY

Silences are awkward. Always speak whilst eating and in this way keep conversation going.

Wait until everyone is seated and ready to begin before eating.

If there is a big group, wait until everyone is seated before sitting. But, if all attending have learned the etiquette, then this takes some time – so arrive early. Someone has to sit first, so make some suggestions – perhaps tallest people should sit first, or suggest that very fat people might need more time to be comfortable.

When eating with others, everyone at the table should begin and finish at the same time. The best way to do this is to eat almost everything as quickly as possible, and leave one spoonful to the end.

STOVIES À LA RENÉ

We do not have stovies in Switzerland. I am glad I emigrated – what a wonderful dish. There are many variations of stovies, but they traditionally consisted of whatever meat and gravy was left uneaten from the big Sunday roast, cooked slowly with floury potatoes and other root vegetables on the stove – hence stovies. Stovies, without fail, taste better the day after cooking, but rarely last that long. This version is made using, my particular favourite, lamb mince. Some add sausages but I detest this.

Kelly-Marie's brood have attempted to make stovies using leftovers from a sausage supper. I can tell you this does not work.

250g lamb mince
700g floury potatoes (such as Maris Piper), diced
1 onion, chopped
2 carrots, sliced
100g turnip, diced
About a cup of lamb stock (more if stovies begins to become too dry)
Salt and pepper

Brown the mince. The fat that comes from the mince should be enough to cook the onions in this dish. Add the chopped onion and cook until softened. Add the chopped potatoes and mix thoroughly. Add the sliced carrots and diced turnip and mix through. Heat the stock and pour over.

Season with salt and pepper. Cover the pot and cook over a low heat, stirring occasionally for around 30 minutes or until the potatoes are soft and floury.

Serves four. Bon!

MINCED COLLOPS

The word collops has its origins in France and in the word "escalopes", meaning slices of meat. Traditional collops would use thin slices of beef, lamb or venison. Mince collops uses courser minced meat than normal. Another name for lumpy mince perhaps?

Collops tends to be what they do around here after they have had a glass too many.

500g finely chopped or coarsely minced lean steak
1 onion, chopped
1 teacup of strong beef stock
Salt and pepper
4 poached eggs
Triangles of buttered toast

Brown the minced steak thoroughly. Add onion and fry till soft. Add stock and simmer mince for one hour. Season to taste before serving. Pour into a preheated shallow dish. Top with four poached eggs. Garnish with triangles of buttered toast.

Serves four.

TOAST TIP

The way they like to make toast here is under a hot grill – traditionally, not an eye-level grill. Both sides are blackened, then the black bits are scraped off with a kitchen knife holding the toast over the sink.

Some people leave one side blackened then cover liberally with butter, margarine or a butter substitute.

If you have many guests and little bread, cut it very thinly having removed the crusts. This is called Melba's toast – named after an Australian opera singer Dame Nellie Melba.

Scraping Melba's toast after the blackening process is complete is a skilled operation, and it will probably break. If this happens serve the bits in a bowl and announce them to your guests as "croutons".

MINCE AND DUMPLINGS

Dumplings are a favourite in British cuisine – a wonderful accompaniment to mince. In Scotland sometimes they are called doughballs or doughboys, and I certainly have encountered many doughballs and dumplings in my travels around Britain.

For the mince:
500g minced beef
2 onions chopped
2 carrots chopped
25g flour
Approx. 250ml beef stock or unthickened gravy

For the dumplings:
100g self-raising flour
50g beef or vegetable suet
Salt and pepper
Pinch of mixed herbs
Cold water to mix

Brown the mince and stir to break up lumps. Add the chopped onions and carrots and fry until the vegetables are soft. Add the flour and mix thoroughly. Gradually stir in the stock or unthickened gravy to just cover the mince. Simmer for around 60 minutes.

To make the dumplings: Mix the suet into the flour. Add seasoning. Gradually add water until you have a soft dough. Shape the dough into golf-ball-sized pieces. Place on top of the mince for the last 20 minutes of the cooking time with the lid firmly on. Turn the dumplings halfway through their cooking time.

Serves four.

Opposite: My lovely wife Kelly-Marie is devoted to mince

BEEF HOT POT

I have been often asked by diners at my gourmet restaurant about Betty's Hot Pot and whether this was something I would add to the menu. As a chef who is always interested in finding new exciting culinary dishes I contacted Mrs Betty Williamson of Johnston Street to enquire about her signature dish. Betty kindly gave me permission to use her mince hot pot recipe and it has proved to be very popular with diners. It was only later that I discovered that it was the wrong Betty.

1kg potatoes, peeled and thinly sliced
500g minced beef
1 onion, chopped
2 carrots, sliced
400g tin of chopped tomatoes
1 tbsp tomato purée
1 tbsp Worcestershire sauce
150ml stock
Salt and pepper
25g butter, melted

Brown the mince thoroughly and add the chopped onion, sliced carrots, chopped tomatoes and their juice, tomato purée, Worcester sauce, salt and pepper, and water or stock. Bring to the boil, then reduce heat, cover and simmer for 20 minutes, stirring occasionally.

Line a casserole dish with half of the sliced potatoes. Season. Make sure that the potatoes have been very thinly sliced or you will need longer to bake. Pour in the mince mixture and then cover with the remaining potato slices. Brush the top with melted butter

Bake in the oven for approximately one hour at 180°C, 360°F, gas mark 4. Serves four.

LAMB HOT POT

One-pot dinners such as this is are great favourites in Kelly-Marie's family. They prefer the pot noodle though as they do not have to wash up the pot.

1 kg potatoes, peeled and thinly sliced
500g minced lamb
2 carrots, sliced in circles
4 onions, sliced
250ml white wine
100ml stock
1 tsp chopped fresh thyme
1 tsp chopped fresh rosemary
Salt and pepper

Brown the lamb mince in its own fat (lamb mince often contains a higher percentage of fat than beef mince). Transfer to a plate. Fry the sliced carrots and onions in the oily pan that contained the mince. Add a little vegetable oil if you feel there is not enough fat to cook the onions.

Place half of the onions and carrots at the bottom of a casserole dish, followed by a layer of potato slices. Season with salt and pepper. Add the mince and then the thyme, rosemary and more salt and pepper. Then add the remainder of the onions and carrots. Cover with the remaining potatoes and finally pour in the wine.

Place a lid on the casserole dish and bring to the boil. If you haven't a casserole dish that can be heated on the hob then bring the wine and stock to the boil in a small pan before pouring over the potatoes. Then place in oven for 60 minutes at 180°C, 350°F, gas mark 4. Take the casserole out of the oven and remove the lid. Then cook in the oven for a further 15 minutes at 200°C, 400°F, gas mark 6, to crisp and brown the potatoes.

Serves four.

THE SIDE PLATE

If someone uses your bread plate as their own, do not inform them of their mistake, this would be rude. Use the bread plate on your right as a replacement. This domino effect is spectacular at a circular table.

MINCE REVISITED

When you are looking to give your mince a certain added zing or a petit je ne sais quoi then why not try this recipe for savoury mince. There are various alternative ingredients you can add to the mince, but I highly recommend celery.

1 onion, chopped
2 sticks of celery, finely chopped
500g minced beef
2 carrots, sliced
400g tin of chopped tomatoes
1 tbsp tomato purée
1 tbsp Worcestershire sauce
150ml beef stock
75g garden peas

Brown the mince, stirring thoroughly to ensure it is broken up, and then add the chopped onions and celery, and cook till soft. Then add sliced carrots, garden peas, Worcester sauce, chopped tomatoes and their juice. Add tomato purée, salt and pepper and water or stock. Bring to the boil and then reduce heat, cover and simmer for 30 minutes.

Why not serve with roast wedges of potatoes, roast vegetables and champagne?

Opposite: I visited this mince with a very personal touch
for a family wedding that I catered for

MINCE AND MACARONI

The term "fusion cuisine" has come into vogue in recent years and I have been keen to introduce fusion dishes into the menu at Paisley's premier à la carte restaurant. The whole philosophy of fusion is to bring together different culinary traditions and I have done this by combining two favourite local dishes, mince and macaroni cheese, to make one exciting new one. Although sadly, so far, mince and fish fingers has proved less successful.

250g macaroni
500g minced beef

A simple tomato sauce:
    1 onion, chopped
    1 clove of garlic, crushed
    1 red pepper, chopped
    1 tbsp olive oil
    1 tbsp tomato purée
    500ml carton of passata (or a tin of chopped tomatoes)
    Fresh basil, chopped
    Black pepper
    ½ tsp sugar

Cheese sauce:
    25g butter
    25g flour
    250ml milk
    A small amount of grated strong cheese, approx 25g
    Grated Parmesan cheese

To make the tomato sauce: Slowly fry the onion, red pepper and garlic over a low heat in some olive oil, till soft. Add the tomato purée and cook for a further couple of minutes. Add the rest of the ingredients, stir well, then cover the pan and leave to simmer for around 15 minutes.

Meanwhile, boil the macaroni in boiling salted water until it is cooked al dente, which is approximately 10 minutes but see the packet for suggested timings. Drain thoroughly when cooked.

Dry fry the mince. Add the prepared tomato sauce and cook for 20 minutes. Transfer the mince mixture to a deep, ovenproof dish.

To make the cheese sauce: Melt the butter in a saucepan. Add the flour, mix thoroughly and cook for a few minutes. Remove from heat and add the liquid gradually, beating well. Add seasoning, return to the heat and bring to the boil for five minutes. The sauce should be smooth, glossy, and coat the back of a spoon. Remove from the heat, add the grated cheese and stir till it melts.

Stir your cooked macaroni into the cheese sauce and pour on top of the mince. Sprinkle with grated Parmesan cheese and bake in the oven for 30 minutes at 200°C, 400°F, gas mark 6.

LE MENU

Some dishes will be described in a foreign language. You can probably guess these, so no need to trouble the waiter who has got enough to worry about without being bothered by you.

Beware of lengthy flowery descriptions especially when these involve "served on a bed of anything".

"Drizzle" is a weather condition, not a method of cookery.

Hot dishes will be described as *table d'hote* or *haute cuisine*.

Dishes served from the trolley will be *à la carte*.

Ignore the specials – because these are leftovers and will be very old and not tasty bites. By choosing from the menu you ensure that your dish of choice is very fresh unless it happens that it is the special – so it is better that you don't know.

Always order water from the tap – that is what goes into the fancy bottles anyway.

Encourage other diners to order the same dish because this will mean that the cooking time is the same and that dishes will simultaneously arrive.

Bread and rolls are usually free (if you are spending enough) and should be torn apart with your fingers, never cut with a knife. Get to the butter dish as soon as possible so you have enough.

PART TWO

UBIQUITOUS MINCE

THERE is more to mince than fantastic minced beef. Minced lamb, minced pork and even minced turkey are all mouth-watering alternatives.

And although there is nothing wrong with comforting mashed potatoes, you can also consider rice or pasta or potato wedges. Or you could be more adventurous and try a wonderful mince casserole or a hearty pie. Why you could even consider a salad as a side-dish. A Glasgow salad is perfect.

And if you find that you have made more of your mince dish than required for one sitting, then, no problem. Simply cover your leftovers with cling film, pop in your fridge and reheat thoroughly the following day. It will still be delicious. In fact, some would argue that second-day mince is the best. Or, you could do as I do, throw it out after three days, feeling less guilty that you have at least attempted to keep it. Alternatively, you could give your leftovers to a family pet or relative.

The world of mince is truly your lobster – although having once had to cook mince and lobster together for a customer, I would not recommend it at all.

La crème de la mince!

Opposite: A triumph in food fusion once again,
with my mince-and-tatties mini pizzas. Bella!

BEEF CAKE

I once heard the term "beef cake" spoken by some of the female diners in the restaurant. It was shouted at my head waiter Serge. He and I did not know this dish they were demanding. I was curious about what it could be. I managed to find a traditional recipe which I have adapted and the dish has proved to be very popular, especially with the ladies who always smile when Serge gives it to them.

500g minced beef
100g bacon or ham
1 onion, finely chopped
2 sticks celery, finely chopped
75g breadcrumbs
2 tbsps chopped parsley
2 tbsps tomato purée
25g butter, melted
½ tsp mixed herbs
Salt and black pepper
2 eggs, beaten

Chop up the bacon or ham into very small pieces. Sharp scissors make this an easy job. Mix with the mince in a bowl. Add the onion, celery, butter, breadcrumbs, parsley and tomato purée and mix together well. Add the herbs and salt and pepper. Add the beaten eggs to bind the mixture.

Place in a foil-lined 2lb loaf tin or mould mixture into a loaf shape, wrap in foil and place in a roasting tin.

Cook in oven at 190°C, 375°F, gas mark 5 for 75 minutes. Take out of oven, pull back the foil and then cook for a further 15 minutes.

Serve cake in slices. Can be eaten cold with salad.

Opposite: The Mince Master Deluxe microwave, a model I will happily endorse for home cooking when I become a celebrity chef

BEEF BEANPOT

Another dish that has proved very popular in my restaurant. From time to time I'm sure I have heard the word Beanpot shouted at me when I am out and about in Paisley, presumably by satisfied diners recognising my idiosyncratic dress sense.

1 tbsp vegetable oil
500g minced beef
2 onions, sliced
2 carrots, sliced
1 stick celery, chopped
1 tbsp cornflour
400g tin tomatoes, chopped
4 tbsps red wine
300ml beef stock
Salt and black pepper
1 tin mixed beans (drained weight 255g)
50g cheese, grated

Brown the mince in a frying pan in its own fat, stirring to break it up. Remove the mince from the pan and place in an ovenproof dish.

Heat oil and fry the onions, carrots and celery in the frying pan for a few minutes to soften and then add to mince.

In a bowl, blend the cornflour with a little beef stock until smooth, then add the tomatoes and their juice, the red wine and the remaining stock. Transfer to a small pan. Continue to stir as you bring to the boil and add the salt and pepper. Then pour into the dish with the mince and vegetables.

Cover the dish and cook for 45 minutes at 180°C, 350°F, gas mark 4. Add the drained beans and cook for another 15 minutes.

Remove from oven and sprinkle grated cheese on top. Retrun to oven to melt the cheese. Serves four.

COMPLAINTS

If a problem arises about the food or service, complain loudly.
It is essential that other diners are warned.

STUFFED ONIONS

In ancient Egypt, onions were an object of worship, and symbolised eternity. One of the earliest cultivated crops, they are less perishable than other foods and easily transportable by bicycle. Conscious of the importance of reducing Maison de Mince's food miles, I usually send Serge to the cash-and-carry on his BMX to get ours.

6 large onions
2 tbsps vegetable oil
1 celery stick, chopped
350g minced lamb
50g mushrooms, chopped
1 tsp thyme, chopped
25g fresh breadcrumbs
Salt and black pepper

Peel the onions, trim the roots but leave the top. Cook for 10 minutes in simmering water until soft but still intact. Drain the water and leave to cool

Cut off the tops of the onions about a quarter of the way down. Spoon out the centre of the onions and chop this finely.

Cook the lamb mince, celery, mushrooms, chopped onion, salt and pepper and thyme in oil in a pan until the mince is thoroughly browned. Add the breadcrumbs. Fill the onions with the mince mixture and place upright in an oven dish. Cover the dish with foil and the cook in oven for 35 minutes at 190°C, 375°F, gas mark 5. Serves six.

WINE

The wine list is no place for snobbery and jargon. Most people have a preference for red or white wine. Some extremely fat and greedy people say they like to have both. This is why rosé was invented by the Portuguese.

The year on the label is not generally a sell-by date, but some of these wines should have been disposed of before now.

STUFFED MUSHROOMS

"Life is too short to stuff a mushroom", so said Shirley Conran in 1975. All I can say is her mushrooms must have been too wee. Choose big, manly-sized mushrooms that will accommodate big, manly portions of pork mince.

4 Portobello mushrooms
100g minced pork
1 lemon rind, grated
Salt and black pepper
1 tbsp breadcrumbs
2 tbsps sage, chopped
Olive oil
1 tbsp parsley, chopped
60ml plain fromage frais or soured cream

Remove the stalks from the mushrooms and chop very fine. Brown the minced pork, stirring regularly. Add in lemon rind, chopped mushroom stalks, salt and pepper, breadcrumbs and sage, continuing to stir.

Take your de-stalked mushrooms and brush with some olive oil. Divide the mince mixture between each of the 4 mushrooms and fill evenly. Cook for 15 minutes at 180°C, 350°F, gas mark 4. Spoon fromage frais on top of each mushroom, sprinkle with chopped parsley and serve.

WINE

Red wine should be served at room temperature – which will vary depending whether you are in Siberia or the Sahara.

White wine will be served chilled – so you can't tell if it is a bit "off".

Opposite: The cellar of Maison de Mince. Brown or red (tomato) sauce? The eternal controversy rages on

BAKED POTATOES WITH SPICED LAMB

I know my signature dish involves the mashed tattie, but we like baked potatoes at Maison de Mince. The potato is humble but beautiful. It makes me cry when I think about what some people do to potatoes or when I have to make Serge clear the crisp bags from the doorway of Maison de Mince of a morning.

When you peel a potato you lose fibre, iron and calcium along with the skin. You wash it and rinse away carbohydrates, some vitamin C and minerals. When they make crisps they additionally destroy B vitamins and then add a generous proportion of fat, salt, artificial flavourings, colouring and preservatives! So, compared with the beautiful innocent potato that you started off with, you end up with 50 times the fat, 20 times the salt, a third of the iron, fibre, vitamin C and thiamin.

150g minced lamb
8 good-sized baking potatoes
1 onion, chopped
1 garlic clove, crushed
1 tsp cinnamon
½ tsp allspice
½ tsp turmeric
2 tbsps tomato purée
Salt and black pepper
100ml vegetable stock
1 tbsp crème fraiche

Pierce the potatoes and brush with oil. Bake in oven at 200°C, 400°F, gas mark 6 for about 60 minutes or until tender.

While baking the potatoes, brown the mince in its own fat. Add the garlic, cinnamon, allspice, turmeric, tomato purée, salt and pepper and mix well. Then add the stock and simmer for 30 minutes, stirring regularly.

When the potatoes are baked and have cooled slightly, slice off their tops and hollow out the insides. Put the potato insides in a bowl and mash with the crème fraiche. Then spoon the mash back into the potatoes, leaving enough room to top up with the spiced mince.

Return to the oven and cook for approx 20 minutes or until piping hot.

Serves six

LAMB CASSEROLE

420g tin of haricot beans, drained
225g streaky bacon
2 onions, sliced
2 cloves garlic, crushed
500g minced lamb
150ml vegetable stock
1 tbsp tomato purée
400g tin of tomatoes
1 bay leaf
Salt and black pepper
¼ tsp marjoram

Cut the bacon into small pieces using scissors. Fry the bacon until crisp in a cast-iron casserole pot. Remove the bacon then fry the onions and garlic in the bacon fat until soft. Add the mince and stir until brown. Mix the mince, bacon, beans, and vegetable stock in the casserole pot. Add tomatoes and their juice, tomato purée, marjoram, bay leaf and salt and pepper.

Bring to the boil then cover and transfer to the oven for 90 minutes at 180°C, 350°F, gas mark 4. Check regularly and add more stock if required.

Serves four.

ACCIDENTS DO HAPPEN!

If you spill salt, this is very bad luck. You need to throw more over your left shoulder to stop the demons.

DEEP-FRIED MINCE

Ha ha. Only kidding, well kind of. Thai-style, minced prawn and pork, deep-fried won tons, with a delicious coriander dipping sauce. Go easy on the fish sauce!

Won tons:
250g pork, minced
250g prawns (fresh or cooked), minced
4 water chestnuts
2 shallots, finely chopped (or you could substitute about 4 spring onions)
2 tbsp soy sauce
1 tsp fish sauce
1 red chilli, deseeded and finely chopped
A packet of (defrosted) frozen won ton wrappers (available from Chinese supermarkets)
6 mushrooms

Dipping sauce:
1 tbsp fish sauce
2 tbsps rice wine
2 tbsps white-wine or rice vinegar
4 tbsps water
1 tbsp sugar
1 tsp ginger root, finely chopped
1 clove garlic, finely chopped
1 red chilli, deseeded and finely chopped
2 tbsps finely chopped fresh coriander

For the filling: In a food processor, mince together the pork, prawns, water chestnuts, mushrooms, shallots and chilli. Add soy sauce and fish sauce and mix. Take a won ton wrapper. Place about half a teaspoon in the centre of the skin. Wet around the edge and draw the pastry together to make a little parcel. Press firmly. Deep fry the won ton in vegetable oil until lightly browned.

For the dipping sauce: Combine the fish sauce, rice wine, rice vinegar, water and add sugar. Heat and mix till dissolved. Taste. Add more sugar if preferred. Add more water if too salty for taste. Allow to cool a little. Add chopped garlic, ginger, chilli and coriander and leave to infuse in fridge for a couple of hours. Serve the won tons hot, and the dipping sauce chilled.

Opposite: With Oriental mince I always serve a "fortune tattie" at the end of the meal

STUFFED PEPPERS

4 red peppers
2 tbsps vegetable oil
1 onion, chopped
350g minced beef
50g mushrooms, chopped
450g tin of baked beans
2 tbsps tomato purée
Salt and black pepper

Slice off the top of the red peppers and take out the core and the seeds. Put peppers in boiling salted water for 3 minutes before washing them in cold water. Drain all water and leave peppers standing upside down.

Heat the oil in a frying pan and fry onion for 3 minutes. Add the mince and cook until browned. Add mushrooms, baked beans, tomato purée and salt and pepper and bring mixture to the boil.

Fill the peppers with the mince mixture and place the peppers standing upright in an oven dish. Cover the dish with foil and cook in the oven for 45 minutes at 190°C, 375°F, gas mark 5. Serve with rice. Serves four.

CHOOSING DISHES

Always choose something mincey as this is very easy to digest and unlike the steak or the lamb it is easier to talk with your mouth full.

STUFFED MARROW

Stuffed marrow is a simple but tasty dinner-party dish. If the marrow is exceptionally big, cut across it widthways into approximately 4 cylindrical portions (depending on the size of the marrow). Cut about 2cm from the top to make a little lid for each one, scoop out the seeds inside, steam it briefly, stuff it with mince and roast it. Then, you can serve an invividual stuffed marrow portion for each guest, rather than cutting slices from the whole stuffed marrow.

If you serve up a whole stuffed marrow to each of your guests they will surely remember it for years to come.

1 medium-sized marrow
250g minced beef
50g fresh breadcrumbs
50g mushrooms, finely chopped
1 onion, finely chopped
2 tomatoes
1 tbsp tomato purée
25g melted butter

Brown the mince then add the onion and mushroom and cook until the chopped onion is clear and soft. Add the tomatoes and tomato purée and continue to cook, stirring thoroughly for a further 10 minutes.

Wash and peel the marrow. Halve it lengthways and scoop out the seeds. Steam cook the marrow until not quite tender, then place it in an oiled roasting tin.

Add the breadcrumbs to the mince mixture and then pile the stuffing into one half of the marrow, then cover with the other half. Brush the marrow surface with the melted butter and bake at 190°C, 375°F, gas mark 5, for 20 minutes until completely tender.

This tastes good with a tomato sauce like the one in the mince and macaroni recipe on page 40.

MINCED BEEF WITH PASTA

500g minced beef
2 red peppers, thinly sliced
1 tbsp olive oil
1 tsp fennel seeds
6 garlic cloves, chopped
Salt and black pepper
400g tin tomatoes
150ml red wine
350g courgettes, halved and sliced
350g penne pasta
25g fresh basil
Parmesan cheese, grated

Brown the mince. Add the onions, fennel, garlic and salt and pepper. Stir regularly until the onions and garlic are soft. Add the tomatoes and their juice, and the red wine. Simmer for 20 minutes. Add courgettes and peppers and cook for another 5 minutes.

Meanwhile, cook the pasta in salted boiling water for about 10 minutes, or according to the packet instructions. Drain pasta. Add the mince mixture, basil and black pepper, stirring well. Simmer for another 3 minutes and sprinkle with Parmesan cheese.

THE PATRON SAINT OF MINCE?

Saint Lawrence , d. 258 AD, is the patron saint of cooks, comedians, fire prevention, France and the poor. I think this also qualifies Lawrence to be the patron saint of mince!

STEAK TARTARE

Trained as I was in France, I was keen to introduce some of the best of French cuisine to the good folk of Paisley, and, realising how keen they were on minced beef I was sure that they would enjoy steak tartare. Regrettably, however, I have discovered that even the diners at my own gourmet restaurant were not enamoured of ordering a dish whose main ingredient is raw mince, no matter how much of a delicacy it is in France. Not even changing the name to "steak tartan" persuaded my clientèle to try it.

Beef tartare, consisting of finely chopped raw steak or high-quality beef mixed with various herbs and spices, goes back to Russian medieval times.

The Tartars shredded their meat and ate it raw – no wonder they invented a sauce to take the taste away.

One small step for mankind – a dropped splodge of chopped raw steak onto the fireplace – and "Hey Bisto™! Hamburgers!"

500g fillet steak
3 egg yolks
4 tbsps olive oil
2 tbsps parsley, chopped
Salt and black pepper

Take the fillet steak and trim and mince very finely. Mix in the egg yolks, oil, parsley and salt and pepper. Shape. Et voilà!

BEEF AND PARSNIP PIE

This wholesome bake goes down well in my à la carte restaurant, despite the funny tasting tatties on the top.

Parsnips are root vegetables related to carrots. Until the potato came along, its place on the platter was often occupied by the parsnip – just like the Romans who occupied much of Europe in the days of their Empire.

The parsnip comes from the Mediterranean, and originally grew to the size of what we would consider a baby carrot. The Romans thought that parsnips were aphrodisiacs and the legionnaires were delighted that the further north they came the bigger their parsnips grew. This is why the Romans kept marching and came to Scotland.

1 onion, chopped
2 carrots, chopped
500g minced beef
2 tomatoes, peeled and sliced
Salt and black pepper
150ml beef stock or unthickened gravy
1kg parsnips
50g butter
25g grated cheese

Brown the mince and cook until browned. Add the onion and carrots and cook till they begin to soften. Add the tomatoes, salt and pepper and stock or gravy. Increase heat and bring to the boil then reduce heat and simmer for 15 minutes.

Peel the parsnips, cut into even-sized pieces and cook in boiling salted water until tender. Drain the water and mash parsnips until soft and smooth. Beat in butter and black pepper to the parsnip mash.

Pour the mince into a dish and spread the mash on top. Sprinkle with grated cheese. Bake in oven for 30 minutes at 200°C, 400°F, gas mark 6. Serves four.

Opposite: Our mince delivery. We go through a lot of mince at the Maison

SPAGHETTI BOLOGNESE

Spaghetti Bolognese, or spag bol as it is affectionately known, is not generallly served up in Italy. In Italy the meat-based sauce, or *ragù*, from Bologna would be served with tagliatelle or lasagne.

People add all sorts of things to their Bolognese sauces that are not authentic, such as mushrooms, beans, spices, chicken pieces ... but even "authentic" sauces will vary from Italian mama to mama. It's a sauce that really invites a dash of this and handful of that. Addition of herbs is also not "authentic" in Bolognese sauce but I think it tastes nice.

I have found spaghetti Bolognese to be a very popular dish in Britain, and believe it is regarded as the exotic alternative to mince and tatties.

3 rashers streaky bacon
1 onion, chopped
1 clove garlic, crushed
2 carrots, finely chopped
2 sticks celery, chopped
500g minced beef (or veal)
400g tin of tomatoes
1 pint passata
1 tsp sugar

150ml beef or vegetable stock
150ml red wine
2 tbsps tomato purée
Salt and black pepper
Pinch dried oregano
2 bay leaves
450g spaghetti
Grated Parmesan cheese
Fresh basil

Cut the bacon into small pieces with scissors. Fry the bacon in a pan until it starts to crisp up. Add the mince and continue to cook until it is browned. Add the onions, carrots, celery and garlic and cook until vegetables are soft. Then add the tomatoes and their juice, passata, sugar, stock, red wine, tomato purée, herbs and salt and pepper. Cover and simmer for at least 60 minutes.

Cook the spaghetti in salted boiling water according to packet instructions. Drain the spaghetti when cooked and divide between the plates. Remove the bay leaves. Add the Bolognese sauce to each plate and finally sprinkle each plate with grated Parmesan cheese and chopped fresh basil. Serves four.

MINCED LAMB CRÊPES

100g plain flour
1 egg, beaten
250ml light ale
Olive oil
1 onion, chopped
500g minced lamb
150ml chicken stock
1 red pepper, seeded and diced
1 green pepper, seeded and diced
Salt and black pepper
Vegetable oil for cooking

Sift flour into a bowl and add a pinch of salt. Make a hole in the centre of flour and break in the egg. Gradually add the light ale, beating the mixture to form a smooth batter.

Fry the onion in oil until soft. Add the minced lamb and continue to cook until brown, stirring regularly. Add stock, peppers and salt and pepper, bring to boil and then reduce heat and simmer for 10 minutes.

Heat some oil in a frying pan and pour in a little batter to make a thin coating of batter in the pan. Cook until underside of batter is brown. Turn or toss and cook the other side. Remove pancake from pan and follow the same process with the rest of the batter. The mixture should make around 10 pancakes.

When the pancakes are ready, lay all of them flat and divide the mince filling between them. Roll the pancakes around the filling.

Place in an ovenproof dish. Cover with foil and place in a hot oven, 200°C, 400°F, gas mark 6, for 15 minutes until piping hot.

Could be served with a simple tomato sauce (see page 40).

Opposite: Mince can be the personification of sophistication

PART THREE

BURGER ME, IT'S MINCE AGAIN

GENGHIS Khan and his Mongols may have invented the burger, tenderising raw meat patties under their saddles for breaks between invasions, but the hamburger took its name not from ham, but from the German city of Hamburg (where the Beatles cut their teeth on many a hamburger). The hamburger was a minced meat patty that was popular in Germany for centuries before, in the 19th century, German emigrants travelled to America, taking their beach towels and patties with them.

In 1885, in America, Dr James Salisbury reckoned that the indigestion of soldiers could be controlled by a diet of coffee, and mince in the form of minced meat patties. His recipe was recorded in 1887 as the Salisbury Steak.

By 1912, the hamburger was on a roll, literally, and a culinary ménage-a-trois was born. Old MacDonald had a farm, and now the average burger consumption in America is something like ninety-three hamburgers a week per person ... or something.

The hamburger became one of the most popular dishes in America, so popular that the Americans exported their hamburgers to the rest of the world. But do not be put off by blander brands of pre-packaged burgers. With simple, good ingredients, the burger can be a healthy and delicious dish that is easy to make. Even the roll is optional.

Not that you need be satisfied with just the straightforward classic hamburger. You can add any number of garnishes and condiments to your burger: roast peppers, fried onions, tomatoes, pickles, ketchups, relishes, sour cream or even guacamole are great as toppings. Once, somebody told me that they had even toppped their burger with a pineapple ring, and asked for my opinion. Only one word came to mind – merde!

Aprés le mince,
le déluge

Opposite: Tinned aphrodisiac with mince and King Edward mash adorned with a beetroot crown

67

hhm

Dear Herr La Sagne

Thank you for your kind letter concerning your proposed book project of minced meats of the world.

As curator of the Hamburg Hamburger Museum we would be pleased to contribute to your project, as it was of course here in Hamburg that the hamburger was invented.

The Hamburg Hamburger Museum is extremely proud of the Hamburger and its international influence, and we take every opportunity to educate the world that it was in Germany, and not in the United States that the hamburger was created, centuries before it crossed the Atlantic. And it should be original German hamburgers rather than inferior American hamburgers that should be being enjoyed by millions around the world.

We would therefore like to offer this traditional Hamburg Hamburger recipe to you, for your readers and the good people of Paisley to enjoy. If there is any further information you require about the history of the Hamburg Hamburger and how it is the one true hamburger please do not hesitate to get back in contact.

We would also be happy to give you contact details of our sister museum the Frankfurt Frankfurter Museum if that would be beneficial.

Thank you again for your correspondence.

Otto Graff

Otto Graff
Curator
The Hamburg Hamburger Museum

GERMAN HAMBURGER

This hamburger, served without the bun is called a *frikadelle* in Germany, meaning meatball. And look out for *frikadeller* in Denmark. Shouted with a Scottish accent this sounds somewhat rude.

500g minced beef
3 tbsps breadcrumbs
1 onion, finely chopped
1 egg, beaten
2 tsps of Dijon mustard
Salt and white pepper
Flour for work surface
Oil for frying

Bread rolls
Sauerkraut as topping (onions cut in rings and fried would do if sauerkraut proves unobtainable or unappealing!)

Mix the minced beef and beaten egg together in a bowl with plenty of salt and pepper and the tablespoon of mustard. Add the breadcrumbs to the meat mixture and mix thoroughly.

Heat some oil in a frying pan and fry onion till soft, allow to cool and mix into the mince. Lightly flour your work surface and shape into between six and eight patties of a similar size.

Fry the hamburgers for about 10–15 minutes, turning regularly. The insides must not be pink.

Serve in rolls with sauerkraut or onion and mustard on top.

CHEESEBURGER

There is no written rule that you have to use squares of bland, plastic processed cheese to top a cheeseburger. Of course there's nothing wrong with a good strong cheddar, but why not also try a fine Swiss cheese? There are none finer than the cheeses of my homeland, not even in France. Emmentaler, Gruyère, Berner Alpkäse, Schabziger, Appenzeller, Bündner, Bergkäse, Mutschli, Raclette, Tête de Moine, Vacherin Fribourgeois, Tilsiter, Vacherin Mont d'Or, Formaggini, Gala, Büsciun da cavra, L'Etivaz Tomme vaudoise – ah, if I hadn't discovered the mince I'm sure I would have opened Maison du Fromage!

Did you know that most Swiss cheese does not have holes? Emmentaler is the cheese with the holes. The larger the holes the better the favour. Of the cheese, not the holes.

750g minced beef
2 tbsps parsley, chopped
1 onion, peeled and grated
Salt and pepper
Tabasco sauce, to taste
4 slices of cheese
4 bread rolls or baps

Mix the mince with parsley, onion, salt and pepper and a few drops of tabasco sauce. Divide the mixture into four flattened burgers of equal size.

Grill the burgers for 5 minutes on each side. Cook for longer if you want the burger well done. Place a slice of cheese on top and grill until the cheese begins to melt.

Serve in a roll with tomato slices and lettuce. Serves four.

Opposite: The half pounder with a half pound of cheese, an occasional dish

MUSHROOM AND BEAN BURGERS

In recent years, there has been much debate and discussion in this country concerning good nutrition and healthy eating, especially in relation to what children are being given to eat. There are many television programmes explaining the benefits of a balanced and healthy diet and why it is important to buy as many celebrity cookbooks as possible. I quite agree.

It is of paramount importance to get kids interested in healthy food, and these burgers are a great way to hide from them that they are consuming vegetables and beans.

2 tbsp vegetable oil
4 onions, diced
1 clove garlic, crushed
200g mushrooms, very finely chopped
300g (or a tin) mixed beans, minced or processed
1 tsp cumin
½ tsp white pepper
1 heaped tbsp tomato ketchup
1 tbsp soy sauce
1 slice bread, crumbed
Salt and pepper to taste
Oil for frying

Fry the onions and garlic in olive oil until onions are soft and clear. Add the cumin and mushrooms and continue to cook. Once the mushrooms are cooked, set aside and process the beans in a food processor, or mash with a potato masher.

Add the fried mushrooms and onions, ketchup, soy sauce, salt and pepper and the breadcrumbs to the beans. Mix until thoroughly combined.

Flour your work surface and shape the mixture into patties. Heat about two tablespoons of olive oil and cook for about 3 minutes on each side. Alternatively, brush with oil and cook on an oiled baking tray in the oven at 200°C, 400°F, gas mark 6 till the outsides are browned.

Leftover, cooked burgers can be frozen and reheated at a later date.

VENISON BURGER

It seems very extravagant to mince venison, non? Not at all. Venison can be a tough and potentially dry meat if overcooked. Mincing tenderises, and yet retains the beautiful, gamey, venison flavour. The red onion helps keep the meat moist.

I served these up to my challenged-of-palate nephew-in-law and he said, "Yer burgers ur aff". This means: "I am slightly concerned about the expiration date of your merchandise", which I take as high praise indeed coming from him.

500g minced venison
1 beaten egg
Black pepper
Pinch of salt
25g fresh breadcrumbs
1 tbsp freshly chopped parsley
1 red onion, finely chopped
Oil for cooking
Redcurrant jelly

Mix the mince with the beaten egg, seasoning and parsley. Mix the breadcrumbs in thoroughly. Fry the onion till soft and allow to cool before mixing into mince and breadcrumbs. Then divide the mixture into four equal-sized patties.

Heat the oil in a frying pan and place your raw burgers into the pan. Cook the burgers over a medium heat for 8–10 minutes (4–5 minutes each side). Serve with a teaspoon of redcurrant jelly.

WINE

Wine is very expensive in restaurants and the owners will presume that you know about what is available in your local offie on a 3-for-2 offer, or what the wine of the week is in the supermarket. Therefore, they will generally stock wines of which you have never heard, buying bin-ends on their holidays to Calais.

KILTED BURGERS

These get their name from their delicious streaky-bacon skirts. They remind me of my own experience in a kilt at a family wedding – not my own – which I would rather not go into but involves streaking of another kind. Most embarrassing.

500g minced beef
2 tbsps parsley, chopped
4 rashers streaky bacon
Salt and pepper
Mustard
1 tbsp vegetable oil
4 bread rolls or baps

Mix the mince with the parsley and plenty of salt and pepper. Divide into four equal-sized round burgers.

Spread mustard on one side of a rasher. Stretch the rasher, mustard side down around the burger. Heat the oil in frying pan and place your raw burgers into pan. Cook the burgers over a medium heat for about 10–15 minutes. Serve in rolls. Serves four.

MANNERS AT TABLE

Mobile phones, spectacles, keys, handbags, hats, shoes, dogs etc. – anything that is not an essential part of the meal – should not be on the table.

If you have brought your own supply of spirits or wine to supplement the expensive choice from the wine list, keep this under the table, and take care to add to your glass without the other guests seeing.

This is best done by pointing away from the table and saying: "For pity's sake look at that!!" and everyone turns round – this gives you ample opportunity to refresh your glass unobserved. However, do this too often and you may become "the boy who cried 'Wine!' ".

If you are refilling from your own bottle of red wine, do not spill it or the game will be up.

CHAMPAGNE ROSÉ

CHATEAU D'HACHE

Alc. 12% vol.

Maison de Mince

LAMB BURGERS

Lamb mince makes great burgers. For a variation on this recipe, substitute two teaspoons of cumin, or a tablespoon of chopped mint for the rosemary, and serve with tsatziki, see page 91.

500g minced lamb
3 tbsps breadcrumbs
1 tbsp fresh rosemary, finely chopped
1 tbsp redcurrant jelly
2 tsps chives, chopped
Salt and black pepper
More redcurrant jelly

Mix the minced lamb with the breadcrumbs, redcurrant jelly, rosemary, chives and salt and pepper. Divide the mixture into four equal-sized burger shapes. Cook the burgers over a medium heat for 10–15 minutes, turning regularly.

Serve in a bread roll topped with redcurrant jelly. Serves four.

TABLE SETTING

The amount of cutlery laid on a table in a posh place tells you how many courses might be served, and the number of glasses indicates how many different drinks you can hope for.

If you are faced with multiple cutleries, it is best to know that it is placed in the order of its use. So, the first utensil on the far left and right will be used as a pair when eating the first course, etc.

The waiter will generally organise the tools according to what you order. Do not attempt to eat soup with a fork.

PORK AND APPLE BURGERS

500g minced pork
1 small onion, finely chopped or grated
1 cooking apple, finely chopped or grated
1 tsp freshly chopped sage
25g fresh breadcrumbs
Salt and white pepper

Mix the minced pork with breadcrumbs, onion, apple, sage and seasoning. Turn onto a floured work surface and divide and shape the mixture into four equal-sized burgers. Burgers can either be fried or brushed with oil and grilled until browned on both sides and thoroughly cooked. Serves four.

ROMANCING THE MINCE

For romantic dinners at Maison de Mince, I have a set menu for two and a secluded candlelit alcove. See Aphrodisiacs, page 114.

Appetiser
MINCE-STUFFED MUSHROOMS WITH GARLIC IN BUTTER SAUCE

Starter
MINCE SOUP WITH CROUTONS AND ONION

Mains
MEATBALLS IN MUSHROOM SAUCE, WITH HERBS
SURF & TURF MEDLEY OF OYSTER & MINCE, SPICED WITH
SAFFRON AND GARLIC

Afters
CHEESE PLATTER WITH GRAPES, CHOCOLATE, ALMONDS &
HONEY or just say cheese with grapes and Toblerone™.
AFTER-DINNER MINCE

(I also have two tables-for-one for that couple who
are always fighting, but like to eat out.)

TURKEY AND LIME BURGERS

1 lime, zest and juice
500g minced turkey
1 red onion, finely chopped
1 tbsp fresh thyme or 1 tsp dried thyme
Salt and white pepper
1 tbsp olive oil
A little flour for the work surface

Remove the zest from the lime. Juice the lime. Place turkey mince, red onion, thyme, lime zest and juice, oil, salt and pepper into a food processor. Quickly blend. Cover and chill for four hours to allow the flavours to develop.

Lightly flour the work surface and shape the mixture into four burgers. Fry in oil in a frying pan. Alternatively, cook under a grill: preheat the grill, brush the burgers with oil and cook for 10–15 minutes, or until not at all pink inside.

Serve in a wholemeal bap with salad.

TOOLS

Do not rest your cutlery on the edge of a plate, particularly when it is loaded with food. You could hit the cutlery and catapult the contents across the table or beyond. Mince has an interesting pebble-dash effect, and this is how woodchip wallpaper was invented.

In this part of the world it is best not to wave cutlery in the air to make a point.

You should not hold your fork or knife like a dagger, unless the food is particulary tough.

If you drop a used spoon on the floor, pick it up. Give it a discreet wipe on the tablecloth.

Opposite: Breakfast tatties and mince – ideal for dunking toast soldiers

LORNE SAUSAGE

A burger? A sausage? Both? It's flat, but it's unlike any other burger I have ever experienced. Well, it's square for a start. Or, actually, trapezium-shaped, as I pointed out to Kelly-Marie when trying to impress her with my geometry.

The Scots have discovered and invented many fabulous things – road coverings, rubber tyres, waterproof raincoats, radar, the television, penicillin, Lulu – but the Lorne sausage is perhaps the cleverest. Why make burgers and sausages round when you can make them flat and square, making more efficient use of grill and frying pan space?

The Lorne sausage is a traditional delicacy that is also called sliced sausage in Glasgow and the West of Scotland, and square sausage in the Highlands and the East of Scotland. Or is that the other way round? Whatever. The Lorne sausage contains either minced beef, minced pork or a mixture of the two, it contains a high percentage of breadcrumbs or rusk, giving it a slightly crunchy texture when cooked. When is it best eaten? Breakfast, brunch, lunch, or any time of day if your hangover still persists.

This recipe makes quite a lot but you can slice and freeze small portions. Alternatively, you can just go to the supermarket or butcher and buy some.

500g minced beef	1 tsp salt
500g minced pork	1 tsp white pepper
1 egg, beaten	1 tsp nutmeg
1½–2 cups of dry breadcrumbs	1 tsp ground coriander seed
or crushed rusk	Water

Mix the beef and pork mince together. Mix in the beaten egg and add enough breadcrumbs to make a firm mixture. Add the salt, pepper and spices and mix thoroughly. Add some water if the mixture is a little too firm. Form the sausage into a long cuboid shape. Place in the freezer for a short time but do not allow to freeze. This is simply to solidify the mixture enough to allow it to become easier to slice cleanly.

If you are freezing the Lorne sausage once it is sliced, cut squares of greased paper or cellophane and place between each sausage slice and place a few in each freezer bag.

Fry each slice of sausage until golden brown and crusty on each side and serve in a warm, buttered bap with fried onions.

Opposite: Square sausage is reputed to be a hangover cure

PART FOUR

THE SHAPE OF MINCE TO COME

WHEN you think of mince you invariably think of mince and tatties and shepherd's pie and other hearty and filling main courses that are the *pièce de résistance* of the evening meal. However, there is much more to mince than just big plates of wonderful food.

Mince can be also be shaped to make a myriad of fantastic appetisers, starters or crowd-pleasing entrées for buffets at home, at the office or for that perfect party. For example: meatballs accompanied by a range of savoury dips, and that perennial favourite, sausages on cocktail sticks stuck in a grapefruit.

You cannot go far wrong with meatballs or meat loaves. There are many types of meatballs from around the world that you can try (Greek, Swedish etc.) and many types of sauces that compliment the meatballs.

With meat loaf you will need a loaf tin or appropriate-sized cake tin for the meat loaf mixture. Meat loaf is a very versatile dish with many different ingredients that you can use in the mixture. Meat loaf is also a dish that some people serve cold, but personally I would do anything with meat loaf (but I won't do that!).

Entertaining with mince is almost an art form in itself as you can use any number of garnishes to make the dish more attractive and impress your guests, but you must always remember that the mince is the key and you should not hide your mince away.

Remember, when preparing mince for a party or large group that most mince dishes require the guest to use a fork, so make sure you have enough forks available. Eating meatballs by hand can prove tricky.

You might also consider my meaty meatball soup recipe – so filling that the very thought of a second course on top might just be too much for your groaning stomach to take. Sacrebleu!

If you do decide to go for a mince appetiser or starter it is generally recommended that you do not have mince for your main course, however there are no hard and fast rules and who is to say what is too much mince?

Cherchez la mince!

Opposite: After-dinner Mince. Well if that Blumenthal man can make bacon and egg ice cream ...

MEATBALLS

There are hundreds of different types of meatball recipes for you to enjoy. Almost every country in the world has their own meatball speciality and you can find lamb meatballs, pork meatballs and beef meatballs that have been fried, boiled, roasted or steamed.

Chinese meatballs are usually made from pork and are steamed or boiled. Pork balls can be found in soup and steamed beef balls can be served as dim sum. Spanish meatballs are called *albondigas*. They are served in a tomato sauce and are thought to have originally been a Moorish delicacy. Mexican albondigas are served in a soup with vegetables.

Greek meatballs are called *keftedes* and are made with onions and mint. In Turkey, meatballs are called *kofte* or *kofta*, and there are many delightful meatball recipes found throughout the Middle East.

Danish meatballs are made from fried pork and are called *frikadeller*. Swedish meatballs are called *kottbullar* and are made from either beef, or beef and pork, with breadcrumbs and onions. Swedish meatballs have become popular in many places of the world as they are good quality and inexpensive to buy, although some find the instructions quite difficult to follow.

In Britain, the most famous meatballs are faggots, which are very popular in parts of England and Wales. They are usually made with minced pig's liver or heart, and so, some unadventurous people will say that they are not sure they like the idea of faggots, but once they have tried them with peas and gravy they are usually converted.

Opposite: My Divot Surprise caused a sensation when I catered for the Open at Royal Troon

M René La Sagne,
Proprietor,
Maison de Mince,
Paisley.

Dear René

Fantastic to hear from you again. It was only the other day that I was playing golf with Rhys from the Bank and talking about how we would have to organise another trip up to Scotland. I know that Bryn from the Lonely Lamb Tavern is up for it, as well as Gareth the Post, Gethin the Fish and Richard the IT consultant. Might go east this time and try the links courses of Fife, but never fear we will still have time for a trip west to Paisley's premier gourmet restaurant. To this day, everyone still talks about that bread and butter pudding you made with custard and prunes. Never tasted anything like it.

I think that the book on mince is a cracking idea and I am delighted that you have asked me to be your Welsh contributor. Made me feel very proud.

Of course there are many cracking mince ideas from Wales, both from minced lamb and minced beef, but if I had to choose one and one only then it will have to be faggots.

Yes I know that some people are put off faggots by the fact that they are made from pigs' hearts, liver and other off-cuts, but if any other country knows not to be put off by what something is made from it is the haggis-loving Scots. And faggots with peas and gravy is a true Welsh delicacy enjoyed by thousands of Welsh men, women and children on a daily basis. As my daughters Charlotte and Catherine would say, faggots are lush.

Keep in touch, René, and if you ever fancy trying real Welsh faggots then come on down. The boys are keen for a return golf tournament and Charlotte and Catherine are very keen to meet you, although I should let you know that neither of them are fond on prunes.

All the best,

Dai Davies

WELSH FAGGOTS

500g minced pig's liver
110g breadcrumbs
1 onion, chopped
50g shredded suet
½ tsp dried sage

Mix the minced liver, breadcrumbs, onion, suet and sage together. Divide and shape the mixture into eight equal-sized meatballs. Bake in oven for 45 minutes at 190°C, 375°F, gas mark 5.

Serve with gravy and peas.

THE NAPKIN

A napkin can be used to wipe your mouth and catch the spillage as you eat. If you are a particulary messy eater and have to take care of your clothes – perhaps you have to take them back to Marks's in the morning – you should carry your own bib with you, rolled up in your pocket, and have a waiter assist you by tying it round your neck.

Once seated, you will find in some establishments that a head waiter will take your napkin, shake out the French fold, and place the napkin, unfolded, on your lap. If this happens, it means that he thinks you are in a restaurant for the first time and don't know what it is for. Leave it there until you are finished unless it is required for mopping purposes, having tucked it in securely to part of your clothing.

VIKINGA
INTERNATIONELL
KOTTBULLAR

Dear Monsieur La Sagne

Thank you for your letter concerning your proposed book project *Mince Of The World*.

We would be delighted to contribute to such a project, as Swedish meatballs have been eaten throughout our history and we believe that there is nothing finer, not even reindeer meat, than a plate of Swedish meatballs, or kottbullar, served with gravy, potatoes and lingonberry jam.

We in Sweden have a long history of exporting the best of Sweden to the rest of the the world – Greta Garbo, Ingmar Bergman, IKEA, Volvo, Bjorn Borg, Henrik Larsson. And Swedish meatballs are probably the most popular meatballs in the world and are enjoyed throughout Scandinavia, Europe and North America as well as Sweden itself.

We hope that our recipe for kottbullar is what you were looking for and that meatballs are a dish that the people of Paisley will enjoy. Best wishes with the book project and as another famous Swedish export ABBA once said "Thank you for the music and thank you for the meatballs."

Yours sincerely,

Frida Malmo

Frida Malmo
Commercial Manager
Viking International Meatballs
Stockholm

KOTTBULLAR
OR SWEDISH MEATBALLS

For the meatballs:
100g butter
1 onion, chopped
2 tbsps evaporated milk
100g breadcrumbs
750g minced beef
1 egg beaten
Salt and black pepper
1 tsp parsley, chopped

For the gravy:
3 tablespoons flour
The rest of 1 large tin evaporated
  milk
1 cup beef stock
½ tsp salt
¼ tsp black pepper
Pinch paprika
Chopped fresh parsley

Melt 25g of the butter in a frying pan and fry onions for 5 minutes or until soft. Remove the onions from pan and add to the breadcrumbs in a bowl.

Pour two tablespoons from a large tin of evaporated milk into the bowl and mix with the breadcrumbs. Stir well and leave aside to soak.

Mix the mince, breadcrumbs and onion, beaten egg, salt, black pepper, and parsley and onion together. Once well mixed, start making golf-ball-sized meatballs.

Heat the remaining butter in a the pan and add the meatballs. Cook for 15 minutes, turning regularly, until meatballs are browned on all sides and cooked thoroughly. Remove the meatballs from the pan, leaving the butter and meaty bits in the pan.

To make the sauce: Add the flour to the drippings in the frying pan and mix till smooth. Slowly add the rest of the evaporated milk and the beef stock. Bring to the boil, stirring until smooth and creamy. Add salt, pepper paprika. Cook for 5 minutes. Strain, add parsley and pour over your meatballs.

Serve with lingonberry jam.

KEFTEDES
OR GREEK LAMB MEATBALLS

Keftedes are flattened meatballs. Simply roll into a golf ball shape and then squash. But not too much. Very therapeutic.

500g minced lamb
25g breadcrumbs
1 egg, beaten
1 tsp ground cumin
1 tbsp mint, chopped
1 tbsp parsley, chopped
1 tbsp lemon juice
2 spring onions, chopped
Salt and black pepper

Mix together all the ingredients thoroughly. Shape into golf-ball-sized meatballs and then flatten on a floured surface. You should get around 15 meatballs. Place in an oiled roasting tin and cook for 15 minutes at 220°C, 425°F, gas mark 7 or until meatballs are well browned and thoroughly cooked.
   Serve with sour cream or tsatziki.

TSATZIKI

500ml Greek yogurt or sour cream
1 cucumber, finely diced
4 cloves garlic, crushed
2 tbsps olive oil
1 tbsp vinegar
1 tsp fresh dill, chopped
Salt and pepper

Dice the cucumber very finely. Strain it tightly using a muslin cloth to get rid of excess moisture. Mix together with all the other ingredients.

MEATBALL RAGOÛT

500g minced lamb
2 tbsps Parmesan cheese
1 tbsp chopped rosemary
4 tbsps breadcrumbs
2 tsps olive oil
150g turnip, diced
1 onion, chopped
2 carrots, chopped
2 sticks celery, chopped
250g mushrooms, thinly sliced
4 garlic cloves, finely chopped
200g lentils
Salt and black pepper
750 ml vegetable stock

Mix together the mince, breadcrumbs, cheese and rosemary. Shape the mixture on a floured surface into around 12 equal sized meatballs. Heat the meatballs in the olive oil for 5 minutes until they are brown all over. Remove meatballs from pan.

Add turnip, onions, carrots, celery, mushrooms and garlic to the pan and cook until vegetables are soft. Add lentils, stock and salt and pepper, and increase heat to bring to boil. Then add meatballs, cover, reduce heat and simmer for 45 minutes or until lentils are soft.

THE NAPKIN

Once you are finished eating, and there is no food left, place the napkin folded loosely to the left of your plate, where, if one is a dribbly type, it can dry.

If you need to leave the table, perhaps for some emergency during the meal, place the napkin on the chair, unless it is badly soiled, in which case slide the chair under the table.

Opposite: Sausage and mash – my tribute to the Matterhorn

MEATBALL SOUP

Yes, this really is a mince soup. From Mexico.

250g minced beef
3 tbsps breadcrumbs
50g butter
1 onion, chopped
1 clove garlic, crushed
½ tsp mixed dried herbs
2 tbsps parsley, chopped
Salt and pepper
1 egg, beaten
1.25 litres beef stock

Fry the onions in a little of the butter or until soft. Put the mince, breadcrumbs, herbs, garlic, parsley and salt and pepper in a bowl and mix thoroughly. Once cooled, add the onions. Add the egg to bind the mixture.

On a floured surface, shape the mixture into small meatballs.

Put the remainder of the butter in a pan and fry the meatballs until they are browned all over. Remove the meatballs from the pan and drain on kitchen paper.

In a separate pot, bring the beef stock to the boil. Then place the meatballs into the pot, reduce heat and simmer for 10 minutes.

Serves four to six.

CHILLI MEATBALLS

350g minced lamb
1 celery stick, chopped
50g breadcrumbs
2 red chillies, de-seeded and finely chopped
2 tbsps chives, chopped (or cut with scissors)
Salt and black pepper
1 tsp olive oil

Mix together the mince, celery, breadcrumbs, chillies, chives and salt and pepper. Shape the mixture on a floured surface into around 20 equal-sized meatballs. Heat the meatballs in oil for 5 minutes or until they are browned all over and thoroughly cooked.

Alternatively, these meatballs could be placed on soaked wooden skewers to make kebabs. In which case, cook under a hot grill or over a barbecue, turning frequently until well browned and thoroughly cooked in the centre.

THE NAPKIN

Ladies can push a corner of the napkin into the cleavage, and, where the cleavage is ample, the napkin can be further secured by jamming it in with a wine cork, or other handy prop.

Ladies who have an extremely large chest area with the bosom resting on the table itself, may have difficulty in actually seeing the plate in front of them. A vanity mirror positioned carefully in the prongs of a dessert fork can often be helpful.

Gentlemen can secure their napkin between the buttons of a shirt, or keep it tucked behind a fastened collar and tie.

Be careful not to tuck the edge of the table cloth into your shirt or waistband by mistake, because when you stand this will be upsetting – everything will follow you to the toilet.

GEFILTE FISH

Although there are many recipes for delicious fishcakes utilising the flaking of cooked fish, the only recipe I know of that involves minced raw fish is that wonderful classic of the Jewish Passover kitchen, gefilte fish. These fish patties are cooled in the broth in which they were cooked and then served cold with some jellied broth or with horseradish sauce.

Fish balls:
1 lb fresh white fish (cod or haddock is fine), deboned
1 onion, chopped
1 carrot, chopped
1 tsp sugar
1 egg
½ tsp salt
½ tsp freshly ground black pepper
2 tbsp matzo meal (ground up matzos – you could use breadcrumbs if your dish is not for Passover)

Broth:
1 onion, chopped
1 carrot, chopped
Black pepper
Enough vegetable or fish stock to poach the fish patties in a large pot

For the fish balls: Cut fish into manageable chunks and process in a food mixer until smooth. Take half of this mixture and process again with the chopped onions and carrot and a spoonful of sugar. Add this to the other half of the minced fish with the egg, salt, pepper and matzo meal or breadcrumbs. Blend thoroughly.

For the broth: Fry the vegetables in a small amount of oil in a deep pot till soft. Add the stock and bring to the boil, then lower the heat and simmer.

Shape the fish mixture into golf-ball-sized balls or oblong-shaped patties. Drop the balls into the simmering broth. Cover and simmer for about 1 hour, occasionally turning the balls with a spoon.

Remove the pot from the heat and let the balls cool in the broth. Use a slotted spoon to remove the balls. Strain the broth through some cheesecloth and pour over the fish. Makes about 12 patties.

Dear Mister La Sagne

My name is Harvey P. Effenberg III and I am writing to
you after reading an article about your book project in
the magazine Ground Meat World of which I am a regular
subscriber and contributor.

I currently have the great honour and privilege
of holding the post of President of the Ground Meat
Association of Milwaukee having succeeded my father
Harvey P. Effenberg II, who had himself succeeded his
father, my grandfather, Harvey P Effenberg I, who
founded the Association in 1922.

We at the Ground Meat Association of Milwaukee are
immensely proud of our long and illustrious history
for promoting and enjoying top quality ground meat and
we would like to offer to you my grandfather, Harvey P
Effenberg's, meat loaf recipe that he left in perpetuity
to the Association on his passing away in 1963.

I truly hope that you and the good people of Paisley
appreciate the recipe as much as we at the Association
have done for many, many years. There is nothing more
American than sitting down with your family and enjoying
delicious American meat loaf followed perhaps by a slice
of blueberry pie. We at the Ground Meat Association of
Milwaukee can think of no more satisfying a meal in the
world, and for that we are truly thankful.

God bless you, and God bless your ground meats.

Harvey

Harvey P. Effenberg III
President Ground Meats Association of Milwaukee

MEAT LOAF

There is more to meat loaf than a larger than life American singer. Meat loaf is made with minced meat (usually beef) that is seasoned and baked in the oven, traditionally in a loaf tin – so voilà, meat loaf.

In America, in the 1930s, at the time of the Depression, other ingredients such as breadcrumbs or oatmeal were added to make the meat go further. You can also add tomato sauce or pasta sauce or strips of bacon as a topping to the loaf.

The dish is generally served hot, but it can be allowed to cool and served cold in slices although many think this is a strange way to use your loaf.

Although meat loaf is usually made with minced beef, you can also use minced pork or minced lamb instead. Many recipes suggest a combination of minced beef and minced pork as it is argued that two out of three ain't bad.

50g butter
2 onions, chopped
2 cloves of garlic, crushed
1 green pepper, chopped
4 tbsps red wine
675g minced beef
750g breadcrumbs

Salt and pepper
2 tbsps Worcestershire sauce
2 tbsps parsley, chopped
2 tsps thyme, chopped
1 tsp tarragon, chopped
1 egg, beaten
1 sliced tomato

Heat the butter in your frying pan and fry the onions, garlic and green pepper until the onions and pepper are soft. Add the red wine and simmer for five minutes.

Use your hands to mix the mince, breadcrumbs, salt and pepper, Worcestershire sauce and herbs together. Stir in the onion mixture and add a lightly beaten egg.

Place the mixture into a greased 1kg tin. Place sliced tomatoes on top and bake for 90 minutes at 180°C, 350°F, gas mark 4.

Can be sliced and served hot or cold with vegetables or salad.

WINE: THE SOMMELIER

A sommelier is a trained and knowledgeable wine steward, who specialises in all aspects of wine service.

A sommelier usually wears a massive apron in case he makes an incredible mess opening the wine.

The role is more specialised and informed than that of a wine waiter. The sommelier looks down on an ordinary waiter.

Their main contribution of work is the wine buying, the storage of it sideways, and the suggestion of wines that will best wash down each particular food on the menu. I bet they are paid on commission to sell the slow-moving stock before it goes off.

Sommeliers are sometimes tipsy. The later it is in the evening, the more giggly they become. This is because they taste all the wine that is opened in the restaurant during the course of the evening.

I have heard it argued that the role of a sommelier in fine dining today is on the same level as the chef de cuisine. What nonsense! A professional sommelier is little more than a bottle opener, and with screwtops becoming more popular, his days are numbered.
    Last time I said this I got a black eye from a cleverly aimed champagne cork.

On no account pretend to know about wine when you in fact know nothing. Ask the sommelier to recommend something – he is there to help.

On the other hand, if the sommelier is unscrupulous and knows you know nothing about wines or their prices, he will probably just bring you the dearest one.

MEDITERRANEAN LAYERED MEAT LOAF

The addition of the vegetables, olive oil and oregano makes this a Mediterranean meat loaf. In my next book look out for British meat loaf with the addition of sausage, egg and chips. Bon! Just my little joke.

1 tsp olive oil
2 onions, chopped
2 carrots, chopped
2 sticks celery, chopped
450g aubergine, chopped
8 cloves garlic, chopped
1 green pepper, chopped
1 red pepper, chopped
900g–1kg minced beef
6 tomatoes, peeled, seeded and chopped
4 tsps oregano
125g breadcrumbs

Heat the oil in the frying pan and fry the carrots, celery, aubergine, garlic and green and red pepper until vegetables are soft. Allow to cool. Add the tomatoes, oregano and chopped onion to the mince and breadcrumbs and mix together.

Divide the mince into three. Place a third on the bottom of a greased 1kg/2lb loaf tin, then cover with half of the prepared vegetables. Place the next third of the mince on top of the vegetables. Cover with the remaining vegetables and top with the last third of the mince mixture. Press down firmly into the tin and cover with foil. Bake for 1 hour at 180°C, 350°F, gas mark 4.

Can be sliced and served hot or cold with vegetables or salad.

LAMB MEAT LOAF

750g minced lamb
1 egg, beaten
Pinch cayenne pepper
2 onions, chopped
50g fresh parsley, chopped
2 cloves garlic, chopped
1 tsp dried oregano
100g breadcrumbs
4 tbsps Parmesan cheese
2 tbsps tomato purée
2 tbsps red wine

In a bowl, mix all the ingredients together until they are well bound.
    Then spread the mixture firmly into a greased 1kg/2lb loaf dish.
    Bake for 1 hour at 180°C, 350°F, gas mark 4. When cool, cut into slices
and serve hot or cold with vegetables or salad.

ETIQUETTE: POSTURE

When you sit down at first, press heavily on your side of the table, to test that it is a stable table. If it is not, then arrange to take turns eating, or look around for things to put under uneven table legs to make everything solid, such as lawyer's letters or unpaid bills.

If this is not possible, try not to lean on the table. This is a very good reason for choosing mince as it is already cut up for you and easy to eat.

Eaters with a lot of experience can keep their elbows off the table when they are eating. However, when you stop spooning to talk, it is acceptable to rest your elbows on the table and lean forward.

SWISS MEAT ROLL

When I first introduced to the good citizens of Paisley the idea of the popular dish of Swiss meat roll they were delighted as they thought it combined two of their favourite foods. However, once they got over their disappointment at there being no sponge cake involved, they found Swiss meat roll to be an enjoyable alternative to meat loaf.

50g breadcrumbs
1 egg, beaten
1 tsp Worcester sauce
½ tsp mixed herbs
2 onions, chopped
Salt and pepper
750g minced beef
1 tbsp olive oil
300g carrots, boiled and mashed
12 rashers bacon
2 sheets greaseproof paper

Soak the breadcrumbs in the beaten egg and Worcester sauce for 4 minutes. Add the mince, one chopped onion, the mixed herbs and salt and pepper and mix well.

Oil two sheets of greaseproof paper. Turn mince mixture out onto one sheet and make into a rectangle shape. Place another sheet of oiled greaseproof paper on top, with oiled side facing down. Press firmly down with rolling pin until mince is 1cm/½ inch thick.

Heat oil in a frying pan. Add remaining chopped onion and mashed carrots and fry gently. Remove top greaseproof paper and spread vegetable mix on mince. Roll up as you would do a Swiss roll.

Place the bacon rashers on tin foil making sure the rashers overlap. Place the meat roll on top and stretch the bacon over the roll. Wrap the foil around the roll and bacon and seal at both ends.

Place in a baking tin and bake for 90 minutes at 180°C, 350°F, gas mark 4. Take roll out of oven, open the foil on top and then cook for another 20 minutes at 200°C, 400°F, gas mark 6, to make the bacon crispy.

Serve with potatoes, either boiled or roasted.

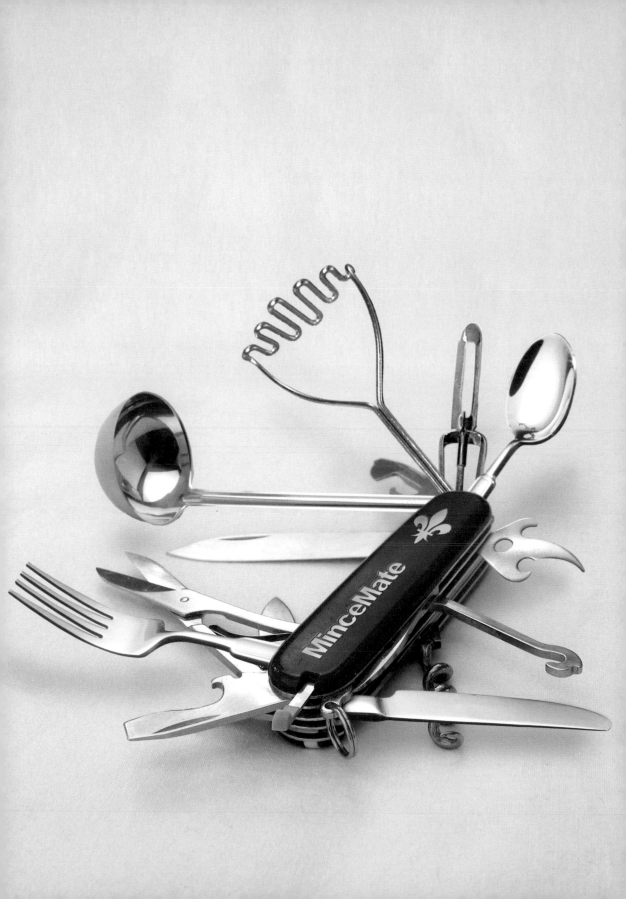

SCOTCH EGGS

Scotch eggs were a delicacy of which I was not aware before I came to Paisley. In my research I have discovered that it appears that the Scotch egg was actually first made in London and is not Scotch at all. Knowing how popular the Scotch egg is with the clientele at my gourmet restaurant I decided to keep this information to myself.

4 eggs
225g pork and beef sausagemeat
75g breadcrumbs or dried fish dressing
1 tbsp parsley
25g flour
1 egg, beaten
Salt and pepper

Hard boil the four eggs in boiling water for 10 minutes. Meanwhile, mix together the sausagemeat with the parsley and divide into four equal portions.

On eggs are boiled, put them in cold water to let them cool. Then remove the shells and sprinkle with flour and salt and pepper.

On a floured surface, take one sausagemeat portion, press out flat and cover an egg with the sausagemeat. Repeat with the other three eggs and three sausagemeat portions.

When complete, brush all four eggs in the beaten egg and then roll them evenly in the breadcrumbs or fish dressing.

Traditionally, Scotch eggs were deep fried, but today's heathier option is to oven bake at 200°C, 400°F, gas mark 6 for 15 minutes, turning halfway through cooking time. Check sausagemeat is thoroughly cooked. These can be eaten hot or cold.

Opposite: A nest of freshly laid Scotch eggs

PORK SAUSAGES

People have been enjoying a good sausage for thousands of years. The Chinese, the Greeks and the Hittites all developed techniques of preserving leftover meat and animal parts within animal intestines. Over the years, the modern sausage of minced or chopped meat and fat became established as a popular delicacy, especially in Europe.

Minced pork is the most popular meat in sausages, but you can also use minced beef, minced lamb or minced veal with spices, herbs, breadcrumbs, rusk or oatmeal added to the mix. Once you have made your sausages they can be cooked, smoked, cured or dried.

Every country in the world has their own native sausage, and some sausages have become famous internationally. In Spain and South America you have the chorizo. In Germany you have the frankfurter, the bratwurst and the knockwurst. In Britain you have the banger and the Cumberland sausage. And in Scotland you have the Lorne sausage.

There are many excellent sausages that you can purchase from your local butcher or supermarket, but you could also consider making your own sausages. Don't worry, no animal intestines need to be involved, and it can prove very satisfying.

500g minced pork
50g shredded suet
100g breadcrumbs
Pinch of salt
1 tsp black pepper
2 tbsps chopped fresh parsley
Pinch ground nutmeg
2 tsps sage
Zest of 1 lemon

Mix together the minced pork, suet and breadcrumbs. Season with salt and pepper and mix in the parsley, nutmeg, sage and lemon zest.

Then, on a floured work surface, simply shape the mixture into whatever sausage shape and size is your preference. Your sausages can then be shallow fried in a little oil or grilled.

Why not try variations with the pork sausage? Omit the sage and lemon and use 50g of fresh chopped apricots and the same of leeks. You might need to use a little beaten egg to hold them together.

Opposite: My Chippolata Tower, a hit at weddings and corporate parties. It's also an amusing Jenga™-style game for children

PART FIVE

MINCE AROUND THE WORLD

THERE are so many great examples of local mince that some people might wonder why they should even bother to try mince dishes from around the world. To this I say *vive la différence* and don't be so bloody boring.

My own experience in moving from France to run one of Paisley's premier à la carte dining establishments has opened my eyes to new and wonderful culinary delights and I feel it is only right that I repay the compliment un peu.

Food is a universal language, and dishes such as moussaka, which we associate with holidays in Greece, can be found in many other European countries. Today, with the advent of so many international restaurants, dishes that used to seem unfamiliar and "foreign food" are now commonplace. Ingredients are easily obtainable, and with a little patience you too can easily produce food as tasty and appealing as that which you might find in your local restaurant.

Some of these recipes require you to make a sauce, but do not let that put you off. These days there are many ready-prepared sauces that the more cautious of you can purchase. Making your own sauces is not as difficult as you may think and will take you further on your international tour de mince.

I have tried to make the recipes as authentic as possible so that they evoke fond memories of sitting at a traditional taverna as you watch the Mediterranean sun go down while tucking into a delicious plate of foreign mince.

Mince sans frontières!

Bruno Conti
Conti's Trattoria
Trastevere
Roma
Italia

Buongiorno René

It was magnifico to hear from you after what has been too many years since we met in Paisley. My cousin Gianfranco gives me all the latest news and tells me that you are making a great success with the gourmet restaurant and that things are going well. Gianfranco tells me that you do a very good minestrone soup, but not as good as his of course. Ha ha.

I think your project on the minced meats of the world sounds fantastic and I am delighted that you have asked me to contribute the Italian recipe. Gianfranco is so jealous. Ha ha!

Of course Italy and Rome are the home of food, the best chefs, the best recipes, the best weather, the best ingredients, the best wine and, yes, the best mince. From the time of the Roman Empire, we have taken our mince through Europe and the Mediterranean and then when Christopher Columbus sailed to America we took our mince to the world. The famous Roman cookbook by Apicius was written in the third century and has many delicious mince recipes and was it not Julius Caesar himself who said "I came. I saw. I ate mince."

It is almost impossible to select only one dish from such a rich and historic tradition, but I give you the Roman Conti family lasagne al forno recipe with my blessing. This varies from the Paisley Conti family lasagne al forno as we do not have the cheddar cheese or the chips. I told Gianfranco that you would only use the recipe in the book and not in your restaurant otherwise we would have to make you an offer that you could not refuse. Ha ha!

I hope you are well, René, and I am sure we will meet again the next time I am in Paisley to see Gianfranco and the family. Good luck with the book and arrivederci for now.

Ciao!

Bruno

LASAGNE AL FORNO

12 sheets lasagne (or 1 packet)
500g minced beef
1 onion, chopped
1 clove garlic, crushed
2 carrots, chopped
2 sticks celery, chopped
400g tin tomatoes
150ml beef or vegetable stock
150ml red wine
2 tbsps tomato purée
½ tsp dried oregano
225g mushrooms, sliced
Salt and black pepper
50g cheese, grated
2 tbsps grated Parmesan cheese

White sauce:
500ml milk
1 bay leaf
4–6 peppercorns
Pinch nutmeg
1 slice onion
50g butter
50g flour

If fresh, cook lasagne sheets in boiling salted water with a tablespoon of olive oil. Drain, rinse and lay the sheets on a clean tea towel to dry. If using dry sheets, follow packet instructions.

Brown the mince, stirring regularly. Add the onions, carrots, celery and garlic and cook till vegetables are soft. Then add the tomatoes and their juice, stock, red wine, tomato purée, mushrooms, oregano and salt and pepper. Cover and simmer for 60 minutes.

To make the white, or béchamel, sauce: Put the milk, bay leaf, peppercorns, nutmeg and onion slices in a separate pan. Bring the mixture slowly to boil, then take mixture out of pan and strain through a sieve into a jug to cool.

Then melt the butter in the cleaned pan, or a different pan, and stir in the flour. Cook for 1 minute. Gradually add the milk mixture from the jug, stirring to make a smooth sauce. When all the milk is added, bring to the boil and cook for 2 minutes, stirring as you go.

Line the bottom of an oven dish with a layer of three lasagne sheets (or as many as it takes to cover it). Then add a layer of the mince Bolognaise, then a layer of the white. Repeat this three more times with the last of the white sauce mixture being your last layer. Sprinkle the top with the grated cheese (such as cheddar) and the Parmesan cheese.

Cook for 45 minutes at 200°C, 400°F, gas 6 or until browned and bubbling.

APHRODISIACS

Aphrodisiacs are named after Aphrodite, the Greek goddess of love who rose from the sea. There is a lady who is called Aphrodite by her thin and frail-looking husband who comes regularly to my restaurant, but I don't think she is Greek. She is certainly not a goddess, and looks as though she falls into the river quite often. We call them Boney and Clyde. They like lots of exotic mince.

Aphrodisiacs are any food, or drink or scent that stimulates desire. Sometimes it is just the shape of something on a plate which is suggestive – asparagus perhaps – it depends on how easily pleased you are. There is much to be said about the power of suggestion.

At Maison de Mince, I have so many sexy suggestions for my customers and I like to keep them regular.

Quince, cheese, chocolate, grapes, walnuts, pine nuts, ginger, avocados, honey ... all are said to have aphrodisiac properties and all can be eaten with mince ... probably. (Note to self: think up mince, quince and honey recipe.)

Garlic and onions – the smell on the breath can backfire. If both partners have smelly breath it's usually OK – as long as it's the same smell.

Chilli – add black chocolate and cheese to your chilli and who can say what will happen? We have so many options with mince to spice things up!

Arugula – sometimes known as Rocket – an aromatic green salad. Very sexy salads are a wonderful accompaniment to mince.

Shellfish – Oysters go down particularly easily, and the zinc content is a substance associated with love. I wouldn't mince oysters – usually, but I never say never – but they go well with beef so one could add them to a beefy stew or delicious mincey pie.

Don't forget artichokes, strawberries, tomatoes, truffles, mussels and of course, ginseng, a Chinese herb. All are sexy foods that can be integrated with dishes which are really mincey ... probably. (Note to self: think up mince, strawberry, truffle and ginseng recipe.)

ALBONDIGAS

500g minced beef
3 cloves garlic, crushed
1 onion, chopped
¼ tsp parsley, chopped
50g breadcrumbs
150ml white wine or vegetable stock
1 beaten egg

Salt and pepper
50g flour
Vegetable oil
400g tin tomatoes
1 tsp granulated sugar
½ teaspoon mixed dried herbs

Mix together the mince, two cloves of garlic, parsley and a tablespoon of white wine or vegetable stock. Then add the breadcrumbs, beaten egg and salt and pepper and mix well.

On a floured surface, make equal-sized small meatballs. Then fry the meatballs in oil until golden brown all over. Remove the meatballs from the pan and drain on kitchen paper. Drain excess oil from the pan, but leave a little to fry the onion and remaining crushed clove of garlic until soft. Add tomatoes, their juice, sugar, herbs and the remainder of the white wine or stock. Bring to the boil and cook for 5 minutes.

Place the meatballs in a casserole dish and pour the sauce over them. Put in oven and cook for 25 minutes at 190°C, 375°F, gas mark 5.

TARJETA POSTAL

ESPAÑA CORREOS

30C

Hola René!
How's it all going? Wish you were here in sunny Marbella. Me and the boys are having a grand time. Weather cracking, golf great. Plenty of sangria and senoritas to keep us occupied – even Wee Jim has stopped moaning! Anyway it was from one of those senoritas that I managed to get that Spanish meatballs recipe you had asked for. There was some confusion at first about what exactly I was asking for, but I wasn't complaining if you know what I mean!
See you soon, Big Al

M. René La Sagne
Maison De Mince
Paisley's Premier Gourmet
Restaurant
Paisley
Near (but not in) Glasgow
SCOTLAND

Dear Mister La Sagne

Greetings to you from Tijuana, on the border between Mexico and the United States, the home of chili con carne, the most popular meat dish in the world.

Chili con carne was the food of the Mexican people in their struggle against the Yankees, the Emperor Maximilian and the dictator Diaz. Pancho Villa cooked chili con carne, Frida Kahlo painted chili con carne and Salma Hayek grew beautiful on chili con carne. When the struggle was over, we Mexicans took chili con carne to the Americanos and then to the world.

So to you, Mister La Sagne, and to the people of Paisley, and to all the readers of your book on the minced meats, be of no doubt that it is Mexico that is the home of the chili and no Yankee chili can compare with true Mexican chili.

So, take our recipe for Tijuana chili and tell the world, and if you are ever in Mexico then visit our cantina and nightclub along the Avenida Revolucion where you can drink Tequila, dance with our beautiful, beautiful dancing girls to the best mariachi music in the world and eat our wonderful chili as the sun goes down over the Pacific Ocean. I do not think even your Paisley can compare with this?

Good luck, René, with your book
and Viva za mince

Emilia Butrobutraguenia

Opposite: A holy trinity of chilli con carne, rice and pitta. Mince, it's a divine thing.

CHILLI CON CARNE

500g minced beef
2 onions, chopped
1 red/green pepper, seeded and chopped
2 cloves garlic, crushed
2 x 400g tins chopped tomatoes
1 tbsp tomato purée
1 tsp cumin powder
2 tsps chilli powder
450g tin red kidney beans
Salt and black pepper
Sour cream
Guacamole

In a large saucepan, fry the mince until thoroughly brown. Then add the onions, cumin powder, chilli powder and peppers, and fry until the onions are soft and then add the garlic.

Add the tomatoes, their juice, tomato purée, and salt and pepper. Simmer for 45 minutes.

Drain the kidney beans and add to the mixture. If your chilli is looking a little dry, add some water. Allow to simmer for another 30–45 minutes.

Serve with rice or pitta bread, or fill taco shells. Top with sour cream and guacamole.

Serves four.

DOLMAS

Dolmas are a minced-lamb-stuffed vegetable dish from Turkey. The vegetable in question is cabbage, cooked for a mere hour and two minutes which should suit British tastes.

2 tbsps oil
1 onion, chopped
100g long grain rice
500ml water
500g minced lamb
2 tbsps parsley, chopped
2 tbsps mint, chopped
2 tsps dill, chopped
Salt and black pepper
12 cabbage leaves
1 carton natural yoghurt

Fry the onion in oil until soft. Stir in rice and cook until brown, stirring regularly. Add water and cook on a low heat until rice is soft and liquid has been absorbed. Leave to cool.

Mix together the mince, parsley, mint, dill and salt and pepper then add to the rice. Mix thoroughly.

Separately boil the cabbage leaves in salted water for 2 minutes. Drain and cut out the stalks.

Spread the cabbage leaves out onto a board and place a spoonful of the mince mixture in the centre of each leaf. Fold the leaf over to make a parcel. Turn parcels over and place at bottom of a saucepan. Pour sufficient water over the parcels to cover the parcels and press down kitchen foil onto the parcels. Cook on a low heat for 60 minutes.

When cooked, remove the foil and take the dolmas out of the water. Serve with yoghurt. Serves four.

ITALIAN MEATBALLS AND SPAGHETTI

A dish from southern Italy that became very popular in America although they had to make the portions much bigger.

500g minced beef
25g breadcrumbs
1 egg, lightly beaten
1 clove garlic, crushed
1 tbsp chopped parsley
Salt and pepper
2 tbsp red wine
1 tbsp vegetable oil
500ml tomato sauce, see page 40 for recipe
1 tbsp Parmesan cheese

Mix together the mince, onion, garlic, parsley, Parmesan cheese, salt, pepper and breadcrumbs in a bowl. Then add the egg and wine. Using your hands, make the mixture into 12 balls.

Then brown the meatballs in the oil in a frying pan. Remove any excess fat when browned. Transfer to a casserole dish and add the tomato sauce. Bake in a covered oven dish at 160°C, 325°F, gas 3 for 1 hour.

Boil the spaghetti in salted water, following the guidance on the packet, and strain and serve. Place meatballs in the middle, sprinkle with Parmesan cheese. Serves four.

SPAGHETTIQUETTE

Spaghetti can be tricky, involving a great deal of twirling, flailing loose ends, flying sauce, staining of clothes and unpleasant slurping. But you must try not to feel self-conscious about eating it in public despite the likelihood of looking like a messy idiot who needs a bib.

You could practise by entertaining at home, serving spaghetti hoops or alphabetty spaghetti. Why not pick out the letters of your date's name, and combining it romantically with yours at the edge of your plate. Best not to get the name wrong.

Zorba's
Restaurant ~ Plaka, Athens, Greece

Bonjour René!

Greetings from beautiful Greece.

It was wonderful to hear from you again, and your letter brought back many happy memories of your visit to Athens all those years ago, and of drinking ouzo as we watched the sunset over the Acropolis. It has been too long, my friend, and you should plan another visit very soon. You are always welcome.

René, I love your idea of a book on minced meats and I am delighted that you have asked myself, and my restaurant to represent Greece. I could not feel prouder at this honour and Elena is very proud as well.

Of course Greece is the home of minced meats. We are the home of democracy, of theatre, of medicine, of literature, of science, of The Olympics and we are also the home of mince. And was it not the Gods themselves of Zeus, Hera, Poseidon, Athena, Apollo, Artemis and Aphrodite who when not feasting on ambrosia on Mount Olympus would be enjoying some delicious Greek minced lamb.

And there could only be one dish and one recipe that I could send you, yes, my very own Georgos Moussaka of the Gods. Moussaka is our national dish and you always kindly said when you came to visit that you had never tasted moussaka as good. I hope the readers of the cookbook will agree.

Thanks again, my friend, for this honour. Myself and Elena wish you all the best. Perhaps we will come and visit you in your new home – I hear Paisley is beautiful, but a little cold perhaps. Until then, we will toast your good health and happiness.

Au revoir, mon ami,

Georgos and Elena Papadopolous

MOUSSAKA

3 aubergines
750g minced lamb
¼ tsp allspice
¼ tsp cinnamon
1 tsp paprika
Black pepper
1 onion, chopped
400g tin tomatoes
1 clove garlic, crushed
2 tbsps tomato purée
¼ tsp oregano
150ml vegetable stock

Topping:
White sauce (see page 113)
or
150ml Greek yoghurt
2 egg yolks
1 tbsp flour
Salt and black pepper
A little grated cheese (optional)

Slice the aubergines, sprinkle with salt and put to one side. Brown the mince with the spices. Add the onion and fry till soft. Add tomatoes and their juice, garlic, paprika, pepper, tomato purée, oregano and stock. Bring to the boil, then reduce heat and cover and simmer for 30 minutes.

Thoroughly rinse the aubergines. In a separate pan, fry them in oil until slices are browned. Drain on kitchen paper.

Place la ayer of aubergines at the bottom of a casserole dish then add a layer of mince mixture. Continue to add layers of aubergines and mince and end with a final layer of aubergines.

Make a white sauce; or try mixing together yoghurt, egg yolks and flour instead. Pour either over the top of the moussaka. Cook for 45 minutes at 180°C, 350°F, gas mark 4 or until brown and bubbling. Will serve up to eight people with salad.

農業

Minister of Agriculture
People's Republic Of China
Food Stuffs Department
Pig and Boar Division
Cantonese Section

Dear Monsieur La Sagne

It was with great appreciation that I received your correspondence concerning your proposed endeavour on the history of minced meats.

We in The People's Republic of China would with great sincerity and respectfulness consider your request for a contribution towards your endeavour as it was of course in the People's Republic of China that the invention of minced meat began and an unparalleled quality and variety of minced meat dishes are to be found.

It is recorded that from the time of the Zhou dynasty the popularity of minced meat as a delicacy began. As our esteemed philosopher Lao Tzu once said in the Tao Te Ching

'There is a thing inherent and natural
Which existed between heaven and earth
Motionless and fathomless
It stands alone and never changes

It pervades and never becomes exhausted
It may be regarded as master of the universe
I do not know its name, if I am forced to give
     it a name, I call
It Mince, and I name it supreme.'

Therefore it is with great humility and history that
we of the People's Republic of China give to your
project and the good people of Paisley our recipe for
Pork Balls as approved by the People's Republic of
China Ministry of Culture and Ministry of Agriculture
and hope that you find it satisfactory.

Thank you again for allowing us this opportunity to
state the People's Republic of China, pre-eminence
in the esteemed world of minced meats, and we
respectfully insist that our historical predominance
is recognised as such in your project.

Yours sincerely,

Chen Wen Yi

Chen Wen Yi
Assistant Deputy Secretary
Minister of Agriculture

CHINESE PORK BALLS

500g minced pork
1 clove garlic, crushed
Salt and black pepper
2 tsps rice wine or sherry
2 tsps soy sauce
½ tsp toasted sesame oil
2 tbsps vegetable oil

Sweet and sour sauce:
225g (approx) tin of pineapple chunks
1 carrot, very thinly cut into matchsticks
1 green pepper, seeded and cut into matchsticks
2 tsps brown sugar
2 tsps soy sauce
1 tbsp cornflour
2 tbsps rice vinegar

For the pork balls: Mix together the mince, garlic, wine, soy sauce, sesame oil and salt and pepper. On a floured surface, shape the mixture into equal-sized, small meatball shapes. Fry the pork balls in vegetable oil in a frying pan until browned all over.

For the sauce: Drain the pineapple and pour the juice into another saucepan. Add the carrot and green pepper to the pineapple juice and simmer for 5 minutes or until the vegetables are soft. Stir in the sugar and the soy sauce. Separately mix the cornflour with the vinegar to make a smooth paste which you should then add to the sauce and simmer for 3 minutes, stirring as you go. Finally add in the pineapple chunks and stir them into the sauce.

Pour the sauce over the pork balls, which should be kept hot, and serve with rice or noodles.

*Opposite: As far as I know, my sushi mince recipe is unique.
Patent pending, which is why I can't reveal the recipe here*

CURRIED BEEF MINCE

1 tbsp vegetable oil
1 onion, chopped
1 tbsp grated ginger
1 red chilli, de-seeded and chopped
1 tbsp curry powder
1 tomato, peeled and chopped
1 tbsp lemon juice
225g green peas, fresh or frozen
1 clove garlic, crushed
500g minced beef
½ tsp allspice
2 tbsps chopped coriander

Fry the onion, chilli and garlic in oil until soft. Add the curry powder and ginger and stir for a few minutes. Add the mince and cook until brown, stirring regularly. Add the tomato and a little water. Cover and simmer for 20 minutes. Add peas and cook at low heat for a further 20 minutes, adding more water if required. Stir in lemon juice, allspice and coriander and cook for a few minutes. Serve with rice. Serves four.

CURRIED LAMB MINCE

1 tbsp vegetable oil
2 onions, sliced
2 cloves garlic, crushed
2.5cm of fresh ginger, peeled and grated
1 tbsp madras curry powder
750g minced lamb
½ tsp turmeric
Pinch paprika
250 ml vegetable stock
Salt and black pepper
150ml natural yoghurt
25g fresh coriander

Fry the onion, ginger and garlic in oil until onion is soft. Add the curry powder, turmeric and paprika and stir for 3 minutes. Add the mince and cook until brown, stirring regularly. Add salt and pepper and vegetable stock. Cover and simmer for 60 minutes. When cooked stir in yoghurt and coriander. Serve with rice. Serves six.

MINCED LAMB KORMA

Korma originates from northern India and is a popular mild and creamy dish. It can be made either as a meat dish or vegetarian dish and korma is often called the chameleon of curries.

1kg minced lamb
½ tsp ground cardamon
1 tsp cumin
1 tsp turmeric
250ml coconut milk
100g coconut, grated
1 tbsp vegetable oil
2 onions, chopped
2 cloves garlic, crushed
4 tomatoes, peeled and sliced
Pinch ground ginger
4 cloves
1 cinnamon stick
1 bay leaf
Salt and black pepper
1 small carton natural yoghurt

Place the mince in a bowl and mix in the cardamon, cumin and turmeric. Cover and place in fridge for 60 minutes.

Fry the onion and garlic in oil until soft. Add the spiced mince mixture and tomatoes and simmer for 5 minutes. Stir in the ginger and cloves and add the cinnamon, bay leaf and salt and pepper. Pour in the coconut milk and grated coconut and bring to the boil, cover, reduce the heat and simmer for 50 minutes. Remove the lid and simmer for another 10 minutes. Take out the cinnamon stick, cloves and bay leaf and throw them away. Stir in the yoghurt gradually but do not heat further or the sauce will curdle.

Serve with rice. Serves eight.

KOFTA

Kofta is a type of meatball found throughout India and the Middle East. It can be made from either minced beef or lamb.

500g minced beef
2 chillies, chopped
1 onion, finely chopped
2 cloves garlic, crushed
Salt and black pepper
1 egg, beaten

For the sauce:
2 onions, sliced
2 tbsps garam masala or mixed spices
2 tsps paprika
500ml coconut milk
2 tsps lemon juice

Mix together the mince, chillies, finely chopped onion, garlic and salt and pepper. Add the beaten egg to bind and shape into golf-ball-sized meatballs. Grill meatballs for 5 minutes or brown all over in a little oil in a frying pan.

To make the sauce: In a pan, fry the sliced onions until soft. Add the mixed spices and paprika and cook for 5 minutes. Stir in the coconut milk gradually.

Add the meatballs to the sauce, cover and simmer for 30 minutes. Add lemon juice and stir. Serve with rice. Serves four.

ACCIDENTS DO HAPPEN!

If you spill something on your dining neighbour, first apologise loudly, then start to clean up the mess as best as you can, by rubbing his or her clothes vigorously, sacrificing your own napkin.

If the spill is really bad, the stained one should excuse themselves and clean it up in the restroom where handy hand-driers can generally be tilted to help dry unsightly damp patches.

FRIKADELLER

Frikadeller are meatballs from Denmark and are often served with red cabbage and lager. Danes say that frikadeller are probably the best meatballs in the world.

2 tbsps breadcrumbs
1 tbsp milk
250g minced pork
250g minced beef or veal
1 onion, grated
Salt and black pepper
1 egg, beaten
Flour
1 tbsp vegetable oil
50g butter

Mix the mince together with the breadcrumbs and milk. Add the onion and salt and pepper and mix together. Add in the egg to bind. On a floured surface, shape the mixture into ten flat rectangular shapes and sprinkle flour on them. Heat the oil and butter in a frying pan and fry the frikadeller for 15 minutes, making sure they are browned on both sides and cooked through.

Serves four with potatoes and gravy, or with cabbage or a potato salad.

SKEWERS

Meatballs are sometimes served on skewers. When cooking with wooden skewers, soak them overnight in cold water so that they don't burn during the cooking process. If there is any burning to be smelled, you want to know that it is your food.

Don't buy skewers that are too thick, otherwise your meatballs will end up looking like Polo Mince.

When eating food cooked on a skewer, the correct procedure is to remove the food from the skewer before eating. Do not ram the whole thing in your mouth sideways, unless you have the correct piercings already in place.

BOBOTIE

Bobotie is a mince dish from South Africa. It has been called the South African equivalent of moussaka, except less creamy, more spicy, and kind of fruity.

25g butter
2 onions, chopped
1 clove garlic, crushed
1 cooking apple, peeled, seeded and chopped
1 tbsp curry powder
1 lemon leaf (a bay leaf would do), whole
500g minced lamb or beef
25g breadcrumbs
Juice of half a lemon
1 egg
1 tbsp chutney
1 tbsp each of raisins and sultanas
Salt and black pepper
1 tsp sugar

Topping:
150ml milk
1 egg

Heat the butter in a frying pan and fry the onions, garlic, curry powder, lemon leaf and apple for 10 minutes on a low heat. Allow to cool. In separate bowl, mix together the mince, breadcrumbs, egg, chutney, raisins, lemon juice and sultanas. Then stir in the cooked onion and apple mixture. Add salt, pepper and sugar.

Transfer the mixture into a greased oven dish and cook for 30 minutes at 180°C, 350°F, gas mark 4.

For the topping: Whisk together the egg and the milk. Remove dish from oven and drain any excess fat from dish. Pour the milk and egg mixture over the top of dish and cook for a further 30 minutes or until brown. Serves four.

KEBABS

I was very surprised to find on my arrival in Scotland at how familiar the locals were with Turkish cuisine. Often I would be told about how no convivial social evening would be complete without sampling a kebab. On investigation, I discovered that the most popular kebabs were the doner kebab (which is meat roasted on a rotating spit) and the shish kebab, which is meat roasted or grilled on skewers. On further investigation I also discovered that, au contraire, not one person that I spoke to had the slightest idea what sort of kebab they had actually had. The "King Kebab" – huge amounts of doner meat served up in a nan bread – is not traditional Turkish food.

750g minced lamb
1 onion, chopped
1 clove garlic, crushed
2 tsps cumin
Salt and black pepper
2 tbsps parsley, chopped
Vegetable oil

Put the mince, onion and garlic into a mincer or food processor and mince twice or until you have a smooth mixture. Stir in the cumin, parsley and salt and pepper and mix together.

On a floured surface shape the mixture into sausage shapes around 8 cm/3 inches long. Place on a plate, cover with cling film and put in the fridge overnight. Soak some long wooden skewers in water overnight.

The following day, thread the kebabs onto skewers and cover with oil. Grill for 15 minutes, turning skewers regularly.

Serve with rice, yoghurt and salad.

RECIPE FOR ROMANCE

The atmosphere for love must be perfect. The room must be comfortable. The room must be warm and free from draughts. If the décor is old or poor, then use low wattage light bulbs, or candles. Maybe you could cook together? Soften the atmosphere? Memorise the recipe but pretend to your partner that you are making it up as you go along.

PART SIX

I SPY A MINCE PIE

THERE are so many different kinds of mince pies for you to get your teeth into, from a festival of meat and gravy, to the Christmas mince pie which has no meat in it whatsoever.

The Christmas mince pie has its origins in the 11th century when crusaders returned from the Middle East with the spices of cinnamon, nutmeg and cloves. These new exotic spices were added to make special mince pies at the festive season with the spices symbolising the gifts brought by the Three Wise Men and making a welcome addition to the taste of minced mutton on its own.

Over the years, the Christmas mince pie became more circular and contained less and less meat. The tradition became that to bring you luck you would eat a mince pie for every one of the twelve days of Christmas, so the mince pies became smaller as well. It was also considered to be bad luck if you refused to eat a mince pie offered to you, so by January 6th you had usually had enough spiced minced mutton to last you for another twelve months.

Today, the mincemeat in a Christmas pie will be a mixture of spices, raisins, currants, sultanas, chopped cherries, grated apples and grated suet, and with sadly not a bit of minced mutton in sight. However, there are many other traditional mince pies and pasties out there that will satisfy all the carnivores amongst you.

Joyeux Mince!

Opposite: Joyeux mince indeed! Mince and tatties is not just for life, it's for Christmas!

MINCEMEAT FOR CHRISTMAS MINCE PIES

Candied peel is normally included here. But it is not my friend. I hate it. I loathe and detest it. Zut! It is the work of the devil. Non. Not nice. If you are so stubborn that you must use it – and I suppose it is traditional – add 200g of the vile substance, reduce the raisins to 400g and the sultanas and currants to 250g each. Ick!

500g cooking apples, peeled, cored and diced small or grated
250g suet, grated
500g raisins
300g sultanas
300g currants
340g brown sugar
Grated zest and juice of 2 oranges
Grated zest and juice of 2 lemons
50g chopped almonds
4 tsps mixed spice
A good glug of brandy (about 8 tbsps)

Combine all the ingredients, except the brandy, in a large oven-proof dish with a lid. Cover the dish and leave overnight. The next day, pre-heat the oven to its very lowest setting. Cover the dish with its lid and place in the oven for 3 hours.

Remove from oven and, as it cools, stir it regularly to distribute the now-melted suet. When the mincemeat is completely cold, stir it thoroughly and add the brandy.

Wash about six large jam jars and lids thoroughly in hot, soapy water. Rinse well, dry them, place them on a baking tray and put in a cool oven, 130°C, 250°F, gas mark ½ (or gas mark 1 if your cooker does not have this mark), for 15 minutes. Remove from oven carefully.

You can now put the mincemeat in the jars and fill to the brim. Cover with waxed discs and put the lids on securely. You may use immediately or keep for up to two years.

MINCE PIES

The fruity, Christmassy variety. For the pastry, I think a little more buttery, crumbly indulgence is necessary at this time of year than the homely half-fat-to-flour recipe. You're going to put on weight at Christmas anyway. Perfect with brandy butter and double cream.

Swiss tart pastry:
250g flour
50g icing sugar
50g cornflour
250g butter

Sieve the flour, cornflour and icing sugar. Cut chilled butter into cubes, add to the flour and using very cold hands (chill them in cold water). Rub the fat into the flour, to make the mixture look like breadcrumbs. Bind it together into a crumbly dough. You should not need to add water because of the pastry's high fat content.

Mincemeat:
225g mincemeat (see page 138)
A bun tin or pie-tray that holds 12
A little icing sugar for dusting

Roll the pastry out thinly. Cut out 12 large rounds and 12 smaller rounds. Line the pie tins with the larger rounds of pastry then, using a spoon, put mincemeat into the pies. Then, cover the pies with the smaller rounds and make a slit on top of each pie.

Bake in a hot oven at 220°C, 425°F, gas mark 7 for 15–20 minutes until pies are golden brown. Dust with icing sugar before serving.

Sheila Bruce
115 Main Street
Balmain
Sydney
NSW
Australia

G'day René,

I hope you do not mind this unexpected letter from sunny Australia, but my Aunt, Margaret Henderson, had written to me about your proposed book on mince and suggested that I might be able to help.

Aunt Margaret lives in Paisley and is always saying how much she and her friend Wilma MacKenzie enjoy dining out at your restaurant and are especially fond of your nouvelle cuisine dishes.

As you would imagine, Aunt Margaret makes a rare plate of mince, and during my last visit to Paisley I was fortunate enough to enjoy my Aunt's mince and tatties on many, many occasions. However, my Aunt suggested that you might like an Australian mince recipe for your book.

I have chosen the Aussie meat pie as my dish – as Australian as kangaroos, koalas and barbies – which can be eaten at any time of day and any time of year, and regularly is.

I hope you find the recipe useful and good luck with your book.

Sheila Bruce

P.S. Don't tell my Aunt this, but I think you have a couple of admirers in Margaret and Wilma. They are also quite partial to your banana fritters.

AUSTRALIAN MEAT PIES

An Aussie meat pie must be small enough to be held in one hand at an Australian Rules Football game. They're usually about 10–15 cm in diameter. They're filled with minced meat and gravy and considered a bit of a national dish in both Australia and New Zealand. The base is shortcrust pastry, the top is puff pastry. There are many Scottish descendants in Australia, I wonder if the Scotch pie is an antecedent of this fellow?

750g minced steak
1 tsp Worcestershire sauce
1 onion, chopped
300 ml beef stock
Salt and white pepper
¼ tsp nutmeg
2 tbsps cornflour
4 tbsps water

Pie bases:
250g plain flour
Pinch salt
50g lard or white cooking fat
50g butter
Approx. 60 ml water (4 tbsps)
Flour for dusting

Pie tops:
375g puff pastry
Milk or beaten egg

Brown the mince in a pan, stirring regularly. Add the chopped onions and fry till soft. Drain away any fat. Add nutmeg, salt and pepper and beef stock. Cover and simmer for 20 minutes. In a cup, add approx 4 tbsps of water to the cornflour and mix till smooth and milky. Add this to the mince and stir. Increase the heat to boil and add Worcestershire sauce, continuing to stir. Reduce heat and simmer for 10 minutes. Let the mince mixture cool.

Make the base pastry by sieving the flour and salt together. Add the lard and butter, cut into small cubes, and rub into the flour using cool fingertips. When there are no lumps of fat left, add sufficient cold water to mix to a stiff dough (approx 5ml/1tsp for every 25g of flour). Knead lightly before rolling out on a floured board or work surface.

Cut out the pastry to line eight 10-cm pie tins. Fill with mince mixture. Roll out puff pastry and cut out lids for pies. Dampen edges of pies and place lids on tops. Seal all the edges and brush with milk or beaten egg. Make a hole in top of the pies and bake for 25 minutes at 200°C, 400°F, gas mark 6.

It is vital to serve with a dollop of tomato ketchup on top!

SAVOURY MINCE PIE

Round these parts, this pie would be called a "mince round". Have a mince round for New Year, some might say. I certainly like to have a mince round.

900g–1kg minced steak
1 potato, diced
500ml water
100ml tomato ketchup
1 tbsp curry powder
2 tbsps Worcestershire sauce
500g puff pastry
1 carrot, diced
1 onion, diced
1 tbsp plain flour
Salt and black pepper
1 egg, beaten

Brown the mince and add the onion, carrot and potato. Cook until vegetables are soft. Add flour and stir well. Gradually stir in the water, tomato ketchup, Worcestershire sauce, curry powder and salt and pepper. Bring to the boil, cover, reduce heat and simmer for 30 minutes. Allow to cool.

Roll out the pastry to line a 25–26cm/9–10-inch pie dish, add mince mixture and dampen pastry edges with water. Roll out the remainder of the pastry to a big enough size to form a lid, and press edges together to seal. Make two slots in the top and glaze with egg. Bake for 15 minutes at 220°C, 425°F, gas mark 7, then reduce heat and bake for 20 minutes at 180°C, 350°F, gas mark 4 or until golden.

COOKING AT HOME AND ... ROMANCE!

If you are planning a romantic dinner, you need something you can cook successfully – so you don't get upset and stressed and throw things – and that can be rescued if it all goes horribly wrong.

The answer? MINCE! And champagne.

Menu

THE WEDDING DINNER OF
Senga AND Boaby

❦

Minced Pork Pâté with Oatcakes
Meatball Pakora with Chilli Dip
Melon with Minced Ginger

❦

Mince
Soya Mince

*Served with seasonal vegetables and boiled or
creamed potatoes*

❦

Mince Pies and Clotted Cream
La Mail d'Arctic

❦

Tea or Coffee
After-Dinner Mince

SCOTCH PIES

The Scotch pie is a delicacy that is usually made with minced mutton. It can sometimes, confusingly, also be called a mince pie. Scotch pies are often served as an accompaniment to a pint in your local hostelry and have become associated with food that you eat at football games, where the tradition, so I am told, is that if you are unfortunate enough to be served a disappointing or undercooked Scotch pie you are supposed to throw it at the referee.

Hot water pastry:
200g lard or dripping
600g self-raising flour
1 tsp salt
250ml boiling water
Milk for glazing

Filling:
400g finely minced beef or lamb
200g finely crushed rusks or fine breadcrumbs
Seasoning of salt, white pepper, and mace or nutmeg to taste
150ml beef stock

For the pastry: In a saucepan, melt the lard in the boiling water. Sieve the flour into a bowl that has been warmed (so that your hot fat and water mixture is not chilled by the flour). Make a well in the middle of the flour and mix in the hot fat and water mixture with a wooden spoon. Once the mixture has cooled a little, knead the dough. When the dough is elastic, leave it in a warm place until it becomes firmer, yet still elastic enough to roll out.

For the filling: Roll out the pastry till it is about $^1/_8$ inch/½cm thick. Cut out rounds that will fit whichever moulds you're using. Then, cut out enough circles from the pastry to make tops for the pies.

In a bowl, mix the mince with the rusk or breadcrumbs. Add stock and bind together, then add the seasoning and mix thoroughly. Fill the pie shells three quarters full, add the tops and seal. Make slits, or little circles, in the pie tops to let the steam out, and brush the pies with milk. Preheat the oven to 200°C, 400°F, gas mark 6. Bake for 25 minutes until golden brown and until the mince is thoroughly cooked.

COUNTRY PIE

A dish originating from the West Country in England, now reborn in the city. Paisley is a city. We have a cathedral. D'accord?

I serve this pie with bits of wheat on the side for extra rural charm.

500g minced beef
1 potato, peeled and diced
2 carrots, diced
1 onion, chopped
100g mushrooms, chopped
Salt and black pepper
150ml cider
225g puff pastry
1 egg, beaten

Mix together the mince, potato, carrots, onion and mushrooms. Add salt and pepper and place the mince mixture in a 1-litre pie dish. Make a hole in the middle of the mixture and pour the cider in.

Roll out the puff pastry and cut away a 2.5cm/1-inch strip of pastry. Wet the rim of the pie dish and place the pastry strip around the rim. Cover the top of the pie dish with the remaining pastry and brush with the beaten egg. Make a hole in the centre of the lid to let the steam out.

Bake in the oven for 20 minutes at 220°C, 425°F, gas mark 7. Then reduce the heat to 180°C, 350°F, gas mark 4 and bake for a further 40 minutes.

FORFAR BRIDIES

The Forfar bridie is a traditional Scottish meat pie or pasty containing beef. The bridie is horseshoe shaped and it said by some to have originated as a wedding meal. This delicious pie comes from the Scottish town of Forfar, or to give Forfar its full name, Forfarfive Eastfifefour.

500g puff pastry
500g beef rump, roughly minced or finely chopped
75g grated beef suet
1 onion, grated
1 tbsp Worcestershire sauce

Mince the beef coursely. Mix in the suet. Grate the onion finely and mix with the beef and suet. Roll out the pastry and divide it into four pieces that are twice as long as they are broad. Place the filling on one half of the pastry, lengthwise, and wet the edges with some water. Fold the remaining pastry over the top and press down firmly around the edges.

Trim and make into horseshoe shapes and pinch the pastry around the edges. Make a small slit in the top to let out the steam while the meat cooks. Let the bridies chill somewhere cool for half an hour to let the pastry rest, then place them on a greased baking tray and bake in an oven preheated to 220°C, 425°F, gas mark 7 for 15 minutes; then, lower the heat to 180°C, 350°F, gas mark 4 for 20 minutes until filling is cooked.

Serve hot, straight from the oven.

CANDLELIT DINNERS

Candlelit dining is very romantic, but problems can arise if care is not taken. Leaning across the table, offering your lips to your partner (perhaps both sets of eyes are closing in anticipation of that lingering kiss) ... to be then disturbed by a tie or sleeve bursting into flames ... disaster! Initially, what seems like the heat of the moment, can quickly turn into a health and safety nightmare!

In romantic situations, always have appropriate extinguishers handy and wear fire retardant clothing.

A MAGNIFIQUE SEVEN-DAY MENU

THURSDAY

SOUP DU LEEK ET POMME DE TERRE

❄

LE SPAG BOL

❄

LA ROLL D'ARCTIC

SATURDAY

LE SAUSAGE DE LORNE, BACON,
FRIED OEUFS,
LE PUDDING NOIR
ET BAKED BEANS

❄

LE THÉ

❄

JELLY AVEC LA SAUCE ANGLAISE

FRIDAY

STICKS DE PAIN AVEC UNE
IMMERSION CHEESEY

❄

GEFILTE FISH

❄

PUDDING DE STICKY TOFFEE

INDEX

Opposite: Dessert

PICTURE CREDITS

Montages by Hugo Breingan

Copyright © 2008 Waverley Books.

Page 63: The Daily Record's front cover "Get your hands off our mince!" is reproduced with the permission of Mirrorpix, Trinity Mirror PLC. Photograph © 2008 Waverley Books.

Page 60: An original photograph courtesy of Photos.com, adapted by Hugo Breingan.

Pages 2, 12, 35, 45, 48, 65, 75, 79, 105, 110, 126, 134, 157 courtesy of PhotoDisc Inc and DigitalVision, and adapted by Hugo Breingan

ACKNOWLEDGEMENTS

René would like to thank the following people for their additional contributions to his book: Ron Grosset, Mike Miller, John Abernethy, Hugo Breingan, Mark Mechan, Penny Grearson, Craig Brown, Eleanor Abraham and Liz Small. Thanks to Bill Abraham for his special spag bol and Hazel Richmond for her granny's plates.